The Lazy Cook's Favourite Food

mouthwatering healthy recipes
for the time-pressured cook

created by

Lazy Cook Mo Smith

®

The Lazy Cook's Favourite Food

Published in October 2004

by

Lazy Cook Mo Smith

Bear House
Bisley
Stroud, Glos. GL6 7BB
Email: info@lazycookmosmith.co.uk
Website: www.lazycookmosmith.co.uk

ISBN 0-9542319-4-5

Written and Edited by
Lazy Cook Mo Smith

Cover Design by Terry Cripps, Gloucestershire
Typesetting by David Onyett, Cheltenham, Glos.
Printed by Leckhampton Printing Co. Cheltenham, Glos.

To

Adam

for his understanding, his
support and his love

To Barbara

With my love,

Mo -

31. 10. 04

Written and Published by the same author

'A Lazy Cook's Christmas'
ISBN 0954231929

Price £4.99 per copy

'Lazy Cook in the Kitchen'
ISBN 0954231910

Price £6.99 per copy

'A Lazy Cook's Summer'
ISBN 0954231902

Price £6.99 per copy

All 3 of the above titles
ISBN 0954231937
Price £13.98

available from

Lazy Cook Mo Smith
Bear House
Bisley
Stroud, Glos. GL6 7BB
(cheques made payable to Lazy Cook Mo Smith)
All prices include p/p.
a percentage of each sale is given to charity

Contents

Bear House

Mo at 'Made in Stroud' day

The Lazy Cook

"Some people eat to live, others live to eat" – without hesitation my family and friends would put me into the latter category – "before you have eaten one meal you are thinking about the next!" But that's how it has always been since, from a very young age, I first experimented with ingredients and became passionate about creating new flavours and putting them into recipes.

Even so, another quote "necessity is the mother of invention" is one which often comes into my mind nowadays. The success of my venture into writing, self-publishing, and marketing my Lazy Cook books has meant that much of my time is now spent out of the kitchen and at my computer. Consequently at the end of the day the very thought of cooking has often been enough to suggest, once again, that we go to one of the village pubs for supper. However, I am at my most creative when pushed for time and this, together with the challenge of overcoming the situation, has driven me on to develop even quicker and lazier recipes which I am now pleased to pass on to you in this new book.

Shortage of time and energy has not meant that I have sacrificed flavours and presentation, these are always in the forefront of my mind when developing a new recipe. I have however, drawn on the increasing number, and improved quality of the prepared ingredients available in the shops and supermarkets. I have taken advantage of all the help I can get to enable me to control, as much as possible, what I eat, and to put together a healthy home cooked meal in minutes.

As many people will already know my recipes are based on healthy eating, using as often as possible, fresh seasonal foods preferably grown in this country. In this book I have gone even further down this road and you will find old favourites such as shepherds pie, steak and kidney pie, stew and dumplings, baked fruit alaska, banana custard and many others, all quickly prepared in my unique lazy cook fashion.

I acknowledge current changes in lifestyle resulting in more people living alone, and the increasing problems of obesity and dieting. I have touched briefly upon each of these subjects, as well as cooking for toddlers and children.

"The more simple it is the more nourishing it is"

Sharing a meal with family and friends remains one of my greatest pleasures, but again these have been pruned to absolute simplicity. The meal begins with the main course, no starter, they are reserved for smart luncheon or dinner parties which rarely happen nowadays. Just one cooked pudding is offered and a selection of fresh fruit. The cheese board is limited to a good Stilton and Cheddar. We all sit around the dining table, or in the garden in summer, with pre-supper drinks and nibbles (usually bought), then I invite our guests to set the table while I put the finishing touches to the meal. It works well, everybody is relaxed and enjoys their contribution to the meal and I am only too happy to have another chore taken away – that is the privilege of The Lazy Cook.

Baking

Cakes and Scones

Additional Biscuit, Buns and Cake recipes can be found in Main Index page 184

Guidelines applicable to this section

When using a food processor

Process ingredients for a few seconds only – food processors are as quick as magic – my reason for constantly using one – very Lazy Cook.

Always process dry ingredients first (flour, baking powder, sugar etc). Then add fat, eggs, milk, or whatever ingredients are included in the recipes.

When a recipe includes dried fruits, or any ingredient which is to be left whole, add these last and process for a very few seconds to mix them in, not to chop.

When is it cooked?

Pastry and Biscuits – when they begin to change colour and become crisp.

Sandwich or shallow cakes – when they rise in the tin and when lightly press in the centre the mixture 'springs' back.

Deeper cakes (including fruit cakes) – when they begin to crack around the edge or in the centre. Test by piercing the centre with a metal skewer, if it comes out clean the cake is cooked.

Cakes

Apple and Sultana Cake – moist and good

225g (8oz) self-raising flour
100g (4oz) demerara (or soft brown) sugar
150g (5oz) margarine – softened
2 large eggs
4 tbls. milk
1 large Bramley cooking apple – peel, core and chop
225g (8oz) sultanas
1 teas. cinnamon powder
a little extra demerara sugar for topping

Set oven at gas 4/180°C/160°C fan/Aga baking oven, 3rd runner down. Drop a parchment cake liner into an 18cm (7″) round cake tin.

Put the flour and sugar into a food processor and process for a few seconds. Add the margarine, eggs and milk and process for a few seconds until smooth. Add the chopped apple and the sultanas and process to mix together. Pack into the lined tin, scatter the top with cinnamon powder and about a tablespoon demerara sugar. Stand the tin on a baking tray and bake in the pre-set oven for 1–1½hrs. or until set (test with a skewer). Remove from oven and allow to cool a little before removing from the tin on to a wire tray. When cold store in an airtight tin.

Lazy Cook tips – *this makes a deliciously moist cake. Use Bramley apples if available – chop them roughly and not too small, finding apple chunks in the baked cake adds to the enjoyment. You may need to add a little more milk to make a smooth mixture. The cinnamon gives a good spicy flavour and the sugar topping adds sparkle. Can be mixed by putting all ingredients into a large bowl and mixing with an electric hand mixer or a wooden spoon.*

Chocolate Vanilla Cake

100g (4oz) plain flour
1 heaped teas. baking powder
50g (2oz) caster sugar
100g (4oz) butter – softened
3 large eggs
$^1/_2$ teas. vanilla extract
50g (2oz) bitter chocolate – grated

Set oven at gas 4/180°C/160°C fan/Aga baking oven, 3rd runner down. Pop a cake liner into a 15cm (6″) round cake tin.

Put the flour, baking powder and sugar into a food processor and process for a few seconds. Add the butter, eggs and vanilla and process until smooth. Spread half the mixture into the lined tin, cover with half the grated chocolate then top with the remaining cake mixture. Smooth the top before covering with the remaining grated chocolate. Stand the tin on a baking tray and bake in the pre-set oven for approximately 40mins. or until set (test with a skewer).

Lazy Cook tips – *I recommend keeping a tin of Charbonnel et Walker, Chocolat Charbonnel in your store cupboard. It may seem extravagant but it is a good quality chocolate, it will save time on grating, and will prevent you eating the remainder of a chocolate bar! The ingredients can be mixed in a large bowl using an electric hand mixer, or a wooden spoon, if you prefer. This is a light and delicious cake without being over sweet. Slice to serve. Store in an airtight tin and eat within 4 days.*

Easter Cake

    100g (4oz) self raising flour
    75g (3oz) caster sugar
    100g (4oz) margarine – softened
    2 large eggs
    1 lemon
    1 x 411g jar lemon curd
    for decoration
    50g (2oz) icing sugar
    1 lemon
    1 fluffy chicken – buy from a cake decorating shop
    egg shell halves
    cake band

Set oven at gas 4/180°C/160°C fan/Aga baking oven, 3rd runner down.

Put the flour and sugar into a food processor and process for a few seconds. Add the margarine and eggs and process for a few seconds until a smooth mixture is formed. Spread the mixture between two 18cm (7″) sandwich tins and bake for 20–30mins. or until set. Turn on to a wire tray to cool. To assemble the cake, remove the zest from the lemon and keep, squeeze the juice over each cake half then sandwich together with lemon curd. Make a lemon cream by processing the softened butter, icing sugar and approximately 1tbls. lemon juice until a smooth, soft consistency (add more lemon juice if necessary), and spread this over the top of the cake. Place the chicken inside the egg shell halves in the centre of the cake and scatter the reserved lemon zest around.

Tie with a yellow or white cake band.

Lazy Cook tips *– the cake ingredients can be mixed in a large bowl using an electric hand mixer, or a wooden spoon. Some of the lemon juice can be stirred into the lemon curd to give a more lemony flavour. The cooked cake can be frozen and assembled and decorated when required.*

Lemon and Fresh Strawberry Sandwich

– serves 8

> 100g (4oz) self raising flour
> 75g (3oz) caster sugar
> 100g (4oz) margarine – softened
> 2 large eggs
> 2 lemons
> 1 x 411g jar lemon curd
> 225g (8oz) fresh strawberries
> 100g (4oz) icing sugar

Set oven at gas 4/180°C/160°C fan/Aga baking oven, 3rd runner down.

Put the flour and sugar into a food processor and process for a few seconds. Add the margarine and eggs and process for a few seconds until smooth. Spread the mixture between two 18cm (7″) sandwich tins and bake for 20mins. or until set. Turn on to a wire tray to cool. To assemble, remove the zest from one lemon and keep, squeeze the juice over each cake then spread with lemon curd and sandwich together with strawberry halves, or slices. Mix the icing to a spreadable consistency with lemon juice and spread over the top of the sandwich. Mark into 8 slices, put a whole strawberry on each slice and scatter the reserved lemon zest in the centre.

Lazy Cook tips *– the cake ingredients can be mixed in a large bowl using an electric hand mixer, or a wooden spoon. The cooked cakes can be frozen and assembled and decorated when required. A delicious cake to serve in the summer.*

New Year Cake

275g (10oz) plain flour
2 heaped teas. baking powder
1/2 teas. ground ginger
100g (4oz) raw cane sugar
175g (6oz) margarine or butter – softened
3 large eggs
1–2 tbls. concentrated orange juice (or fresh orange juice)
100g (4oz) mixed cut peel
100g (4oz) glacé cherries
50g (2oz) crystalised ginger

Set oven gas 4/180°C/160°C fan/Aga baking oven, 3rd runner down.
Pop a cake liner into a 20cm/8″ tin round cake tin.

Put the flour, baking powder, ground ginger and sugar into a food
processor and process for a few seconds. Add the margarine, eggs and
orange juice and process until smooth. Add the remaining ingredients
and process for a few seconds to mix together without chopping the
fruit too much. Pack into the prepared tin, stand it on a baking tray
and bake for 1–1½hrs. or until set (test with a metal skewer). Cool a
little before removing from the tin on to a wire tray. When cold slice
to serve. Store in an airtight tin or polythene bag.

Lazy Cook tips – *the ingredients can be mixed in a large bowl using an
electric hand mixer, or a wooden spoon. Cans of 150ml concentrated orange
juice are useful to have in store for this and other recipes requiring a small
quantity of orange juice. This is a good way of using up left over fruit from
Christmas baking.*

Orange Bran Cake

175g (6oz) butter or margarine – softened
150g (5oz) plain flour
2 teas. baking powder
25g (1oz) bran
125g (5oz) soft brown sugar
3 large eggs
4 tbls. freshly squeezed orange juice

optional topping
100g (4oz) icing sugar
1 orange – zest and juice

Set oven at gas 4/180°C/160°C fan/Aga baking oven, 3rd runner down. Pop a cake liner into a 15–18cm (6″–7″) round cake tin.

Put the flour, baking powder, bran and sugar into a processor and process for a few seconds. Add the remaining ingredients and process until smooth. Pour into the lined tin, stand it on a baking tray and bake in the pre-set oven for 30–45mins. or until set (test with a metal skewer). Remove from oven and leave for a few minutes before removing from tin and cooling on a wire tray. Mix the icing sugar and orange juice to a smooth paste, spread over the cold cake and scatter with orange zest. Serve when the icing has set. Store in an airtight tin, serve within 3 days.

Lazy Cook tips – *can be mixed in a large bowl using an electric hand mixer or a wooden spoon. Concentrated orange juice can be used in the cake, but freshly squeezed is best. Remove the zest from oranges before squeezing.*

Orange and Marmalade Ring – a cake or a pudding

75g (3oz) margarine – softened
75g (3oz) plain flour
1 teas. baking powder
50g (2oz) soft brown sugar
2 large eggs
1 small seedless orange (mandarin, clementine, or similar)
2 good desst. orange marmalade
a sifting of icing sugar – optional

Additional ingredients if serving as a pudding
1 orange – zest and juice
150ml (5fl.oz) double or whipping cream
1–2 tbls. orange liqueur – *optional*
1–2 tbls. ginger wine

Set oven at gas 4/180°C/160°C fan/Aga baking oven, 3rd runner down.

Oil a ring mould. Put the flour, baking powder and sugar into a food processor and process for a few seconds. Peel the orange and break into segments, cut up the peel and add both with the remaining ingredients. Process together then pour into the prepared mould smoothing the top. Stand the mould on a baking tray and bake in the pre-set oven for 25–35mins. or until set (test with a metal skewer). Remove from oven and ease the cake from the ring using a palette knife before turning it on to a wire tray. When cold cut into chunks to serve as a cake. Store in an airtight tin or polythene bag.

Lazy Cook tips – *because the skins of small oranges are thin there is no need to remove the pith. A really good moist cake with good flavours.*

To serve as a pudding – *turn the freshly cooked cake on to a hot serving dish. Remove and keep the zest of a fresh orange, squeeze the juice and pour this into the hot cake. Lightly whip the cream, fold in the reserved orange zest then spoon into the cake cavity, serve any remaining separately.*

If you have a little orange liqueur pour this into the hot cake. The orange juice can be mixed with an equal quantity of ginger wine, heated and served separately as a sauce – a quick and delicious pudding.

Rich Walnut and Almond Cake

225g (8oz) butter – softened
100g (4oz) plain flour
1 teas. baking powder
175g (6oz) soft brown sugar
4 large eggs
100g (4oz) walnut pieces
50g (2oz) ground almonds
1 tbls. sweet sherry

Set oven at gas 4/180°C/160°C fan/Aga baking oven, 3rd runner down. Pop a cake liner into a 15–17cm (6″–7″) round cake tin.

Put the flour, baking powder and sugar into a food processor and process for a few seconds. Add the remaining ingredients and process until smooth. Pour into the lined tin, smooth the top, stand the tin on a baking tray and bake in the pre-set oven for 45mins to 1 hour or until set (test with a metal skewer). Remove from oven and after a few minutes remove from the tin on to a wire tray. When cold store in an airtight tin or polythene bag, or freeze.

Lazy Cook tips – *can be mixed in a large bowl using an electric hand mixer or a wooden spoon – mix the flour, baking powder, sugar, butter and eggs until smooth, stir in the remaining ingredients..*

Serving Suggestions – *a good cake to bake in the Autumn when the new seasons walnuts are available. A good alternative to a traditional rich Christmas cake when I suggest the top is lightly spread with apricot jam or lemon curd, then covered with almond paste. Use recipe on page 11 or buy ready-made. Decorate the top with whole almonds and walnut halves.*

Almond Paste – to cover a 25.5cm (10″) round cake

350g (12oz) ground almonds
275g (10oz) caster sugar
275g (10oz) icing sugar
4 tbls. brandy
2 tbls. fresh lemon juice
1 teas. orange flower water
a few spots almond essence
1 medium sized egg
1 yolk

Mix the almonds and sugars together in a large bowl and make a well in the centre. Whisk all remaining ingredients together, pour into the well and work together to form a paste. Shape, or roll on a surface sifted with icing sugar.

Lazy Cook tips – *try not to over-knead this paste, it will extract the oil from the almonds and will eventually cause a top icing to discolour. Use as soon as it is made otherwise it will become crisp on the surface and difficult to handle. If it is too sticky, add a little more sifted icing sugar; if too dry add a little more brandy or lemon juice.*

Sacher Torte – a Viennese cake which can also be served as a pudding – see Serving Suggestions on page 12.

100g (4oz) butter – soften
75g (3oz) caster sugar
4 large eggs
175g (6oz) bitter chocolate – melted
100g (4oz) ground almonds
1 teas. instant coffee granules – stir into 1 tbls. hot water
Chocolate Icing – *optional* (recipe on page 12)

Set oven at gas 4/180°C/160°C fan/Aga baking oven, 3rd runner down. Pop a cake liner into a 15–17cm (6″–7″) cake tin.

Put the butter, sugar and egg yolks into a large bowl and mix until they are light and fluffy using an electric hand mixer. Stir in the melted chocolate, almonds and coffee. In a separate bowl whisk the egg whites until they are stiff and stir these into the chocolate mixture. Pour into the prepared tin, stand this on a baking tray and bake in the pre-set oven for approximately 45mins.–1 hr (test with a metal skewer). Cool a little before removing from the tin on to a wire tray. When cold store in a covered container in a fridge, or freeze whole or cut into individual slices.

Lazy Cook tips – *a very delicious, rich, moist chocolate cake and even more so with the additional chocolate icing. It is an excellent cake to serve to those who are unable to eat flour or wheat.*

Serving Suggestions – *in small slices!. It is also an excellent standby to serve as a pudding and especially useful if entertaining over a few days – turn each slice on its side and top with a good spoon of whipped double cream and a chocolate truffle (bought).*

Chocolate Icing

> 100g (4oz) bitter chocolate
> 1 teas. instant coffee granules – stir into 1 tbls. hot water
> 25g (1oz) butter

Melt all together and use as directed in a recipe.

Sugar-free fruit cake

225g (8oz) plain flour
2 teas. baking powder
1 teas. mixed spice
100g (4oz) margarine – softened
2 large eggs
100ml (4fl.oz) milk
$1/_2$ teas. vanilla extract
225g (8oz) mixed dried fruit
6–8 walnut halves – *optional*

Set oven at gas 4/180°C/160°C fan/Aga baking oven, 3rd runner down. Pop a cake liner into a 18cm (7″) cake tin.

Put the flour, baking powder and spice into a food processor and process for a few seconds. Add the margarine, eggs milk and vanilla extract and process again until smooth. Add the dried fruit and process for a few seconds only. Pour into the prepared tin, smooth the top and press walnut halves round the edge. Stand the tin on a baking tray and bake for $1^{1}/_4$–$1^{1}/_2$hrs, or until set (test with a metal skewer). Remove from oven and after a few minutes remove the cake from the tin and leave to cool on a wire tray. Slice to serve. Store in an airtight tin or container.

Lazy **Cook tips** *– this cake can be mixed by putting all the ingredients into a large bowl and mixing with a wooden spoon or electric hand mixer.*

Scones

Drop Scones

225g (8oz) plain flour
$^1/_2$ teas. bicarbonate of soda
1 teas. cream of tartar
1 teas. caster sugar
1 large egg
200ml (7fl.oz) milk

Put all ingredients into a processor and process until smooth. Heat a heavy based frying pan and rub the base with a little lard or oil. Drop rounds of the mixture from a dessertspoon on to the pan and when the surface rises and bubbles turn them over using a large metal spatula or fish slice. Cook until the reverse side is slightly browned then remove from pan and keep warm in a clean teacloth until all the mixture is used. Serve, or freeze when cold.

Lazy Cook tips – *the pan should be moderately hot before the mixture is added and it should only be necessary to grease it at the beginning of cooking. Aga users should raise the simmering plate lid for a few minutes to allow it to cool slightly before cooking commences. Vary the size of the scones by dropping the mixture from a table, dessert or teaspoon, dropping it from the tip of the spoon to form rounds, or from the side for an oval shape.*

An alternative method of mixing is to put all the dry ingredients in a large bowl or basin and make a well in the centre. Whisk the egg lightly, stir in the milk and pour this, a little at a time, into the flour well mixing with a wooden spoon until the mixture turns to a smooth paste.

Serving Suggestions – *serve warm or cold spread with softened butter. Work a little cinnamon or mixed spice into the butter to add a different flavour. For savoury presentation spread them with a little cream cheese or pâté and top with salad ingredients or a curl of parma ham, chicken, meat, fish – the choice is yours.*

Scones – cherry, fruit, plain or savoury – *to make approx. 12*

I was taught that scones should be "quick to make and quick to bake".

> 225g (8oz) plain white flour (or 1/2 white and 1/2 wholemeal)
> 2 heaped teas. baking powder
> 1 teas. sugar (caster or granulated)
> 50g (2oz) butter
> 1 egg whisked and made up to 150ml/5fl.oz with milk.

Set oven gas 7/220°C/200°C fan/Aga roasting oven 2nd runner down.

Put the flour, baking powder and sugar into a food processor and process for a few seconds to mix together. Add the butter (cut into small pieces), and process for a few seconds before pouring in the milk mixture until a ball of dough is formed. Remove from the processor on to a lightly floured surface. With floured hands, shape into a round and press down until it is approx. 2.5cm (1″) thick. Cut into rounds using a 4cm (1½″) flutted cutter, place on a lightly oiled baking tray, brush the tops with milk or beaten egg and bake for 5–10mins. or until well risen and brown on top. Remove from oven and cool on a wire tray.

Lazy Cook tips – *sour cream or buttermilk can be used in place of fresh milk. A little extra liquid may be needed when making wholemeal scones. Eat scones the day they are baked. They can be quickly mixed by hand by stirring the flour, baking powder and sugar in a large mixing bowl, rub in the butter pieces and stir in the milk mixture until a dough is formed. (follow instructions for shaping and baking as above).*

Serving Suggestions – *split and serve with jam or marmalade, and whipped cream.*

Cherry or Fruit scones

Add 50g (2oz) glacé cherries or mixed dried fruit to the above recipe.

Savoury Scones

Cheese

Omit the sugar, reduce the flour to 175g (6oz) and add 50g (2oz) grated cheese of a good strong flavour.

Serving Suggestions *– serve hot, split and spread with butter. Alternatively, omit the butter and spread with a spoon of chutney, tomato, or olive pesto. Garnish with a scattering of mustard cress.*

Herb

Omit the sugar and add 2 tbls. freshly chopped mixed herbs. If mixing in a food processor the herbs should be processed before the other ingredients are added.

Serving Suggestions *– serve warm or hot. Split and spread with butter (optional), and fish meat or vegetarian pâté. Sandwich together or leave open. Garnish with a scattering of mustard cress.*

Cooking for One

I am regularly asked for recipes and advice on cooking for one. "It is so boring cooking for oneself" I am told. "What is the point of cooking a roast for one, I get tired of eating the leftovers", I so often hear. In many situations I can understand this, just as I can understand the temptation to buy ready-made meals when time or energy are against you. But surely the same question arises whether we cook for one or for twenty-one – "what shall I cook today"? The boring sameness can cloud mealtimes and finding inspiration is not always easy.

Although I now mostly cook for two, I am in a similar situation to those living alone and especially those in full-time employment. At the end of the day I am tired and hungry and want a meal fast. Whether I am starting from scratch or assembling left-over ingredients the following is how I get an evening meal into the oven in almost as little time as it takes my husband to pour me a drink and set the table. It is what my Lazy Cook philosophy is all about.

"Think big" – whether preparing soups, main courses, vegetables or puddings. Make enough for two or more servings. Eat one and refrigerate the remainder to eat a day or two later. Waste nothing. Even a few tablespoons of liquid left over from a casserole can transform a few ingredients into a tasty meal in minutes. Have a "fridge tidy" every few days – put all leftovers together, top with a few shavings of cheese and bake until hot throughout.

Keep a good "store cupboard". We now have access to a huge variety of ready-prepared ingredients. Stock up with your favourite flavours. They will transform seemingly ordinary ingredients into a delicious meal in minutes saving your time and energy. As you experiment so your skills will develop.

"Plan ahead" – jot down the meals you would most enjoy over the coming few days, buy the ingredients and cook them. We plan for a holiday, why not plan our daily diet?

But what about that Sunday roast? Follow my recipe for Roast Chicken for One on page 131 of this book. Alternatively invite a friend or neighbour round to enjoy a roast, this way you will have company as well as a good meal.

I hope you can see that in addition to freshly cooked single portions of fresh meat, poultry, fish and vegetables, by cooking double the amount you will have in store a variety of home cooked meals which can be heated in as short a time as it takes to cook the potatoes, rice or pasta to go with it. Of more importance, it is a meal over which you have had control of the ingredients you eat and the opportunity to cut down on fats and oils, sugar, salt, and the many preservatives added to bought ready-made meals.

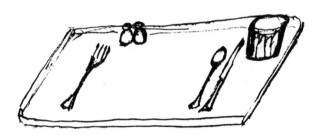

Dieting

I love the story of the lady who, deciding to lose weight, made the usual fresh cream sponge for tea but refused to eat any. The surprised husband said, "why are you not having a slice, are you not feeling well?" "I'm on a diet" said the lady. "What a pity, it's one of the best cakes you've ever made, do have some". "No", was the determined response. But husband, enjoying the cake so much went on to eat half of it. "I will put the remainder in the fridge and you can eat it for tea tomorrow" said his wife.

But ... next morning, when opening the refrigerator for milk for her morning coffee, the lady spied the cake, oh it looked so good, maybe she could taste just the smallest sliver, it wouldn't be noticed. The cake was indeed delicious and one small sliver, led to a slice, then another, and another, until she had eaten all the cake. She then had to make another cake and eat half of that so that she could keep the promised half for her husband's tea!

I can sympathise with this lady. So often I open a box of chocolates intending to eat just one, usually the biggest, but end up eating the lot.

The following are my personal thoughts on dieting and not intended as advice for anyone on a special diet for medical or other reasons.

"We are what we eat" is as true now as ever it was

As I prepare this book there is much in the media about obesity especially among youngsters. We are suddenly being advised that a diet of crisps and coke and other mass produced ready-made snacks is bad for us – please tell us cooks something we don't already know!

Cut down, not out

As is reflected in my recipes, I stress the importance of a healthy and well balanced diet. Our bodies are made up of many parts and each part needs feeding in order for it to function and grow and remain healthy. Carbohydrates, fats, proteins, minerals and vitamins are all essential.

I often recall the lectures given by a dietician when I studied cookery at evening classes. He advised, "think of the food you eat as a repeating pattern of coloured beads. If a colour is missed out, or if too many of one colour are added, the pattern is broken, the diet is unbalanced and the eventual result could well be ill health".

I recognise that in today's world of convenience foods, which we all use in some form or other, this balance is not easily achieved. Even so, it is still possible to enjoy a healthy diet by basing it on fresh seasonal ingredients – the choice is ours. It is worth remembering that the cheaper foods are often the most nutritious. Amongst these are fresh liver and mackerel, tinned whole sardines, salmon and tuna, eggs, cheese, rice and potatoes. In winter cabbage, parsnips, carrots and swedes and in summer tomatoes, cucumbers and all salad ingredients; fruits and vegetables all grown in this country following strict government and EU rules and regulations.

Cut down on the amounts of salt, sugar, oils and fats when preparing meals, they will probably already be included in the packets and tins we keep in our cupboards. Drink lots of water and take a daily walk.

The proportions of food we need depends upon lifestyle, sex and age. I attempt to follow a well balanced daily diet but when I go out to eat, or take a holiday, I eat what I am offered and enjoy it all. When back at home, I revert to my daily diet.

Fish

Guidelines applicable to this section

When is it cooked?

It is difficult to give an exact time for cooking fish because as with other ingredients, it depends on the amount being cooked at one time.

My motto is "undercooked fish is unpalatable, overcooked fish is a disaster". Experience tells me that fish is cooked when it is firm to the touch but there is a little movement. Each flake should be moist. It will continue to cook as it cools. I cook fish at a high temperature.

Nutritional content

Fish is more nutritious and has a better flavour if it is cooked with the skin on. Fish with a high oil content are very nutritious, i.e. mackerel, sardines, pilchards. Tinned whole fish have a high nutritional content and should be included in a weekly diet.

Baked Cod with Grapes Poached in Vanilla and Honey – *serves 4*

700g (1¹/₂lb) fillet of cod
25g (1oz) butter
50g (2oz) fresh or dried breadcrumbs
for the grapes see recipe below

Set oven gas 6/200°C/180°C fan/Aga roasting oven, 2nd runner down.

Cover the base of a shallow ovenproof dish with a film of cold water. Wipe the fish with damp kitchen roll before putting, skin side down, into the dish. Scatter with breadcrumbs and dot with shavings of butter before baking in the pre-set oven for 10–15mins. or until the fish is firm to the touch. Serve straight from the oven on individual hot plates or put down the centre of a hot serving dish. Place the grapes and juices on top and around.

Lazy Cook tips *– the fish can be baked in one piece or cut into portions.*
▊ *Poach the grapes while the fish is baking.*

Grapes Poached in Vanilla and Honey

50ml (2fl.oz) water
1 teas. runny honey
¹/₂ teas. vanilla extract
225g (8oz) green or red seedless grapes

Put the water into a pan, add the honey and vanilla and stir over a gentle heat until dissolved. Add the grapes and simmer gently with lid on pan for 5mins. Serve hot or cold with fish or meat recipes.

Baked Trout with an Anchovy and Tomato Sauce – *serves 4*

> 1 large trout fillet, with skin
> freshly ground black pepper
> little white wine – *optional*
> Anchovy and Tomato Sauce – recipe below

Set oven gas 6/200°C/180°C fan/Aga roasting oven 2nd runner down.

Put a film of white wine or water to cover the base of an ovenproof pan or dish. Cut the fillet into 4 equal sized pieces and add, skin side down. Season with freshly ground black pepper and bake in the pre-set oven for 5–8mins. or until the fillets are firm to the touch. Make the sauce while the fish is cooking. To serve, put the fillets on to individual hot plates or one large serving dish. Serve the sauce separately.

Lazy Cook tips – *if the fillet is cooked in one whole piece it may need longer cooking time- avoid over-cooking, see **Guidelines** on page 22. This is one of the quickest fish meals I cook and is much enjoyed. I call the sauce recipe "the quickest ever tomato sauce" – but it is not just quick to make but also has an excellent flavour – another Lazy Cook favourite.*

Anchovy and Tomato Sauce – the quickest ever!

> 2 tbls. tomato ketchup
> 1 teas. sundried tomato paste
> 4–6 fresh anchovy fillets – crush in a pestle and mortar.
> 1–2 teas. runny honey
> vegetable stock or water

Put all ingredients into a pan and stir over a gentle heat until simmering. Thin down with stock or water to the desired consistency. Serve hot or cold.

Lazy Cook tips – *increase quantities to make a larger amount. An excellent sauce. Always buy anchovy fillets preserved in oil and sold by weight.*

Serving Suggestions – *with any hot or cold savoury food.*

Fish and Bacon Pie – *serves 4*

    450g (1lb) fish fillets
    2fl.oz white wine (or water)
    Parsley and Thyme Forcemeat – recipe below
    8 rashers rindless streaky bacon – cut into 2cm (1″ lengths)

Set oven at gas 6/200°C/180°C fan/Aga roasting oven, 2nd runner down.

Put the wine (or water) into a large shallow ovenproof dish. Add the fish fillets and sprinkle with a little lemon juice. Scatter the forcemeat over and top with the bacon pieces. Put into the pre-set oven and cook for 10–15mins. or until the fish is cooked (please read **Guidelines** on page 22). I like to serve this pie hot or cold with vegetables or salad and a Tapenade Sauce (recipe on page 131).

Lazy Cook tips – *the fish can be broken into flakes or left in whole pieces before cooking. Remove any visible bones.*

Parsley and Thyme Forcemeat

    175g (6oz) bread
    1/2 teas. each dried parsley and dried thyme
    freshly ground white pepper
    1 large egg
    1 lemon – zest and juice

Set oven at gas 4/180°C/160°C fan/Aga baking oven, 3rd runner down.

Break the bread into a processor and process into crumbs. Add the parsley and thyme and process again for a few seconds. Add the egg, the grated zest from the lemon and a little of the juice and process until it blends together. Spread into a lightly oiled ovenproof baking dish and bake in the pre-set oven for 10–15mins.

Lazy Cook tips – *the consistency should be that of a sticky breadcrumb texture. Allow to rest for 30mins. before baking if time allows. Use a good handful of fresh parsley and thyme if available.*

Fish in Batter served with Tomato Sauce

– makes approx. 12

> 150ml (5fl.oz) batter mixture – recipe on page 114
> 225g (8oz) cooked prawns
> little oil

Make the batter in advance. Set oven at gas 6/200°C/180°C fan/Aga roasting oven, 2nd runner down.

Using a 12 hole patti tin, pour a little oil into each hole and put in the pre-set oven for 1–2mins. or until hot. Whisk a tablespoon of cold water into the batter mixture and pour it into the hot fat, $^1/_2$–$^3/_4$ full, and drop a few prawns into each. Return to the oven and bake for 10–15mins. or until well risen and golden. Serve hot from the oven with the sauce (recipe on page 27).

Lazy Cook tips – *these are really quick to make and bake and very delicious. The fillings can be varied i.e. a mixture of shell fish, cod, salmon, haddock etc., also fruit – apple, peach, plum slices.*

Serving Suggestions – *serve 2–3 as starters, or make a quantity and pile them into a dish for people to help themselves – children will love them, a good way to introduce them to 'real' fish.*

Tomato Sauce

tomato ketchup
fresh lemon juice
sundried tomato paste
runny honey

To each tablespoon tomato ketchup add one teaspoon sun-dried tomato paste and and one teaspoon honey. Stir over a gentle heat until hot. If too sharp, sweeten with a little runny honey. Serve hot or cold. Increase quantities to make a larger amount.

Fish Cake *– serves 4*

4 small trout – filleted
4 tomatoes
fresh basil leaves
4 mushrooms – sliced
freshly ground black pepper
6–8 anchovy fillets preserved in oil
1 dash of white wine or water

Set oven at gas 6/200°C/180°Cfan/Aga roasting oven, 3rd runner down.

Put a film of white wine or water in an ovenproof dish or baking tin. Add one fillet, skin side down, and top with tomato slices, freshly ground pepper and basil leaves then mushroom slices. Continuue layering the ingredients until the last fish fillet is added and criss-cross this with anchovies to make a lattice pattern. Drizzle with a little oil before baking in the pre-set oven for 15–20mins. or until the fish is firm to the touch (see **Guidelines** on page 22). Using a fish slice transfer the cake to a serving dish and slice like a cake to serve – hot or cold.

Serving Suggestions – *I like to serve this as a light summer lunch. Accompany it with fresh bread or rolls and a good mixed green salad.*

Fish fillets with Spinach and Parma Ham

– serves 4

> 4 fish fillets
> white wine
> freshly ground black pepper
> 450g (1lb) spinach – cooked (recipe on page 176)
> 8 thin slices Parma or Black Forest ham

Set oven at gas 6/200°C/180°C fan/Aga roasting oven, 2nd runner down.

Put a film of white wine on the base of an ovenproof dish, add the fillets, skin side down, and season with freshly ground pepper. Bake in the pre-set oven for 6–8mins. or until fillets are firm to the touch. Put on to individual hot plates, (or one large hot serving plate). Spoon any juices from the dish over each fillet before topping with the cooked spinach and crumpled ham slices.

Lazy Cook tips – *The flavours and presentation of this recipe are good and quick. The spinach can be cooked while the fish is cooking. If serving with pasta or rice allow extra time for the cooking of these. Parma or Black Forest hams add an instant bacon flavour without needing to be cooked! They will store for several days in a refrigerator and will add instant eye-catching presentation to most savoury dishes and salads – another Lazy Cook ingredient to add to your shopping list.*

Serving Suggestions – *serve with pasta or rice tossed in a little oil and plenty of fresh herbs, and a green salad.*

Fish Fingers

Remove all bones before cutting white fish fillets into strips and place in a lightly oiled shallow ovenproof dish. Scatter with fresh or dried breadcrumbs and top with a scattering of oil. Bake in a hot oven (gas 6/200°C/400°F/Aga roasting oven, 2nd shelf down for 10mins. or until the strips of fish are firm to the touch and the breadcrumbs are turning golden. Cool a little before serving as individual fingers to children.

Lazy Cook tips – *make sure all bones are removed before cooking the fish, even fish bought as 'fillets' often contains a bone or two.*
An ideal recipe to introduce children to fish.

Fish Pâté

Process (or mash) to a paste, one of the following tins of fish – salmon, sardines, mackerel – adding a teaspoon each of horseradish cream, grain mustard, cider vinegar, oil, and 2 teas. sundried tomato paste. Put into a pot/s and store, covered, in a refrigerator or cold larder. Bring back to room temperature, top with curls of anchovy and serve with toast, warm rolls, or bread – a good starter recipe.

Lazy Cook tips – *most tinned fish has excellent nutritional qualities – include them in a weekly diet.*

Fish Pudding – *serves 4*

300ml (10fl.oz) milk
1 medium onion – skin and chop
several good pinches ground clove
freshly ground white pepper
450g (1lb) skinless white fish fillet (or smoked haddock)
2 large eggs
175g (6oz) grated cheese mixed with freshly chopped parsley
6–8 medium slices of bread – buttered

Warm a little of the milk in a pan over a gentle heat, add the ground clove, pepper and prepared onion, place the fish on top and simmer, with lid on pan, for approximately 5 mins. Break the fish into flakes. Butter, or oil, a 1ltr (2pt) soufflé or pie dish, and line the base with buttered bread slices. Top with a layer of the fish and onion (removing it from the pan with a slotted spoon), and some of the cheese, then top with more bread. Continue layering until all the ingredients are used ending with bread scattered with with cheese. Add the remaining milk to the pan juices and warm. Whisk the eggs then whisk into the warmed milk before pouring it through a sieve on to the layered ingredients. Press down with a fork and, if possible, leave for 30mins. to 1 hour before baking in a pre-set oven (gas 4/180°C/160°C fan/Aga baking oven) for 30–40mins. or until well risen and brown on top. Serve hot.

Lazy Cook tips – *make this in a basin if you do not have a soufflé, or suitable pie dish. Stand the chosen dish on a baking tray to bake. Use up odd ends of cheese of mixed flavours grating soft cheeses before hard ones. This recipe can also be made using shell fish.*

Fish Roll served with a Tartare Sauce
– serves 8 slices

325g (³/₄lb) salmon or trout fillet
325g (³/₄lb) monkfish fillet
4 strands of fennel fern
6 rashers rindless bacon
little oil

Set oven at gas 6/200°C/180°C fan/Aga roasting oven, 2nd shelf down.

Lightly oil the base of a shallow baking dish or tin. Stretch each bacon rasher using a blunt knife and place, slightly overlapping on a board (enough to measure the length of the fillets). Top with the fennel fern then the fillets (placed side by side). Enclose in the bacon rashers (like a double sausage roll) and place in the prepared dish, loose bacon ends down. Lightly brush the bacon with oil and bake in the pre-set oven for 20–25mins. or until the roll is firm to the touch in the centre. Remove from oven and when cold slice and serve with Tartare Sauce (recipe below).

Lazy Cook tips – *each fish fillet should be of a similar thickness and length. If necessary, secure any loose bacon ends with a wooden cocktail stick. Can be served hot but slices better when cold. Allow 2 slices per person if serving as a light meal, or 1 slice as a starter. When cold, wrap in greaseproof then foil and store in a refrigerator or cold larder and use within 3 days. Bring back to room temperature before serving.*

Serving Suggestions – *with new potatoes and salad as a main course or, garnish each slice with a little watercress or lambs lettuce to serve as a starter. Serve the sauce separately.*

Tartare Sauce

> 4 tbls. mayonnaise
> 1 tbls. capers – chop roughly
> 1 teas. horseradish cream
> freshly ground white pepper

Mix all together. Serve immediately or store, in a jar, in a refrigerator – use within 5 days. Increase quantities to make a larger amount.

Lazy Cook tips – *recipe for home-made mayonnaise on page 32.*

Mayonnaise – *makes approx. 300ml (10fl.oz)*

> 1 large egg
> 2 desst. wine vinegar
> $^{1}/_{4}$ teas. of each of the following – salt, ground white pepper,
> mustard powder
> oil – approx. 300ml (10fl.oz)

Break the egg into a food processor or liquidiser and add the vinegar, salt, pepper and mustard powder. Process together for a few seconds before gradually pouring in the oil until until it thickens – the more oil you add the thicker it will become. Store in a covered jar and keep in the refrigerator. Use within 7 days.

Lazy Cook tips – there is no susbstitute for home made mayonnaise and with the aid of a food processor or liquidiser it is made in minutes. I use Sunflower oil but others can be used. Different flavoured vinegars can also be used. It is a most useful ingredient to have in store.

Mackerel Fillets with Baked Pear – *serves 4*

> 4 mackerel fillets
> 4 teas. grain mustard
> 2 large pears – peel, cut in quarters and remove core
> 4 tbls. Calvados or Ginger Wine

Put the calvados (or ginger wine) into a pan and bring to boil. Add the prepared pears and simmer, with lid on pan, for 5–10mins. or until the pears have softened. Put a film of cold water into a shallow ovenproof dish and add the fillets (skin side down). Spread the flesh with grain mustard and bake in the pre-set oven, uncovered, for 5–10mins. or until firm to the touch. Serve on individual hot plates or one large serving dish, with the pears and juice on top and around. Serve with rice and a green vegetable of your choice.

Lazy Cook tips – the flavour of the pears is good with this oily fish. Mackerel has a high nutritional value – include it in your weekly diet.

Serving Suggestions – Serve cold in summer with salad and new potatoes.

Paella – *serves 6–8*

2 skinless chicken breasts – cut into strips
2 tbls. oil
2 medium sized onions – skin and chop
1 large red pepper – sliced
1 stalk celery – cut into small strips
350g (12oz) paella rice (or a mixture of brown, wild and camargue)
600ml (1pt) chicken stock
1 clove garlic – chopped
freshly ground black pepper
$^1/_2$ teas. saffron – soak in a little boiling water
several good pinches dried tarragon
16 mussels in shells
175g (6oz) frozen peas – defrost
450g (1lb) cooked prawns – shelled
2 tbls. double cream or 25g (1oz) butter
freshly chopped parsley

Heat the oil in a large pan. Add the chicken pieces and cook for approximately 5mins. or until browning, stirring occasionally, then remove from pan. Add the prepared onion, pepper and celery and cook for a minute, with lid on pan. Put the rice into a sieve and wash under a cold running tap then add to the cooked vegetables. Add the stock, garlic, pepper, saffron and tarragon and stir well. Bring to a simmer, put lid on pan and simmer gently for 15–20mins. or until the rice has softened and absorbed most of the stock. Whilst the rice is cooking prepare the mussels by scrubbing well, discard any that are not tightly closed, and pull away and discard any seaweed-like threads. Add with the peas, and simmer for a further 5mins. with lid on pan. Stir in the chicken and vegetables, the prawns, cream or butter, and cook for a minute or two to heat throughout before serving piled on to hot, individual bowls or one large hot serving dish, and scatter with freshly chopped parsley.

Lazy Cook tips – *a most colourful dish to serve and packed with interesting textures and flavour. A good way of serving fish, poultry and vegetables all in one recipe. The texture of the rice should be soft but not overcooked. The consistency of the finished dish should be moist, more stock may be needed during or after the simmering of the rice, or you may wish to add a little white wine at this stage. The mussels will open as they cook. A good recipe if feeding a crowd. You can be as economical or extravagent as you wish with your choice of ingredients.*

Platter of Smoked Salmon Rolls, Parma Ham and Roll Mop Herrings garnished with Egg Halves and Fresh Strawberries

– serves 8

A perfect meal for summer or for an adult picnic.

> 1 packet smoked salmon – minimum 8 slices
> 1 bunch rocket
> freshly ground black pepper
> 4 large eggs – hard boiled
> 8 fresh anchovy fillets
> 8 thin slices Parma ham
> 8 roll mop herrings
> 8 strawberries – cut in half

Prepare the salmon rolls and eggs as follows – put some rocket leaves on each salmon slice, season with freshly ground black pepper and roll up loosely. Shell the eggs and cut in half then curl a fresh anchovy fillet on top of each half. Arrange these, and the remaining ingredients, in rows on a large platter and garnish with strawberry halves. Serve with salad, new potatoes, mayonnaise and vinaigrette – or as outlined in the 'Picnic in the Park' menu suggestion on page 67.

Salmon Bake – *serves 4–6*

40g (1½oz) butter
1 medium onion – skin and finely chop
25g (1oz) plain flour
300ml (10fl.oz) milk
50ml (2fl.oz) Vermouth or dry white wine
418g tin John West Red Salmon
½ teas. dried oregano (or 1 teas. fresh marjoram if available)
150ml (5oz) single cream
freshly ground white pepper
3 large eggs – hard boil, peel and quarter
175g (6oz) closed mushrooms – wipe and slice
1 tbls. capers – from a jar
50g (2oz) Stilton cheese – crumbled

Set oven at gas 6/200°C/180°C fan/Aga roasting oven, 3rd runner down.

Melt the butter in a large pan, over a gentle heat. Add the prepared onion and cook, with lid on pan, for 1–2mins. or until the onion begins to soften. Stir in the flour and continue cooking for approx. 2mins. Add the milk, wine, juices from the tin of salmon, and herbs and stir until smooth, bring to simmer and simmer until the sauce begins to thicken (1–2mins.). Stir in the cream, season with freshly ground white pepper and remove pan from heat. Put the salmon (broken into pieces), the prepared eggs, mushrooms and capers (strained from the juices), into a large, shallow, ovenproof dish, cover with the sauce and crumble the cheese on top. Bake in the pre-set oven for 20–30mins. or until hot and bubbling.

Lazy Cook tips – *this recipe can be prepared in advance (add the cheese before reheating), – when cold, cover and store in a refrigerator or cold larder. Reheating from cold will take a little longer – even though it might be bubbling around the edge of the dish, test that the centre is also hot by spooning a little out. Other varieties of tinned fish can be included in this recipe, eg. mussels, cockles, shrimps etc. If any are preserved in vinegar, rinse under a cold tap before adding to the recipe. Tinned salmon has a good nutritional value and this is just one of the many ways I serve it.*

Serving Suggestions – *straight from the oven with peas, rice, pasta or warm bread or rolls. A quick family recipe.*

Salmon Steaks with a Melon Cup garnish
– serves 4

> 4 salmon steaks
> freshly ground black pepper
> 4 strands fennel fern – *optional*
> 1–2 tbls. white wine – *optional*
> 4 melon cups – recipe on page 37

Set oven at gas 6/200°C/180°C fan/Aga roasting oven, 2nd runner down.

Put a film of water (or white wine) over the base of a shallow ovenproof dish, add the steaks (skin side down), season each with freshly ground black pepper and top with a strand of fennel fern. Put into the pre-set oven for 10mins. or until the steaks are firm to the touch at the thickest part. Remove from oven, strain off and reserve all the juices. While the steaks are cooling, prepare the melon cups. To serve, put the steaks on to individual plates or one large serving dish and place the melon cups alongside or at the ends.

Lazy Cook tips – *the steaks can be cooked one or two days in advance and stored, covered, in a refrigerator or cold larder. A good combination of flavours and a simple but eye-catching presentation – grand for a summer lunch party.*

Melon Cups – *makes 4*

2 small melons
12 cooked prawns in shells
small bunch red seedless grapes
bunch radishes – leave whole if small or cut into strips
4 fresh mint leaves – cut into thin strips
8 small strawberries

Cut each end from the melons to form 4 cups approx. 2.5cms (1″) deep and remove and discard any seeds. Using a teaspoon, spoon out the flesh into a sieve placed over a basin to collect the juices. Cut a thin slither from the base of each cup to enable them to stand firm and 'hang' 3 prawns from each. To the reserved melon juice add approx. half the flesh, the reserved fish juices, a handful of grapes, several small radishes, the cut mint leaves and strawberries, and stir before packing into the cups. Serve alongside cold cooked fish.

Lazy Cook tips – *all remaining fruit and juices can form the base of a fresh fruit salad. Frozen prawns in shells can be purchased from fish stalls and supermarkets – I recommend several of these are kept in your freezer – they will give an instant, eye-catching garnish to many fish recipes.*

Shellfish with Rice – *serves 4*

225g (8oz) cooked rice – recipes on pages 134/173
$^1/_4$ of a stick of celery – sliced thinly across the stalks
4–6 spring onions – slice thinly, including green stalks
225g (8oz) mix of cooked shelled prawns, mussels, cockles or
  other shellfish of your choice.
collection of freshly chopped herbs
freshly ground white pepper
several pinches curry powder
pistachio nuts – shelled
4tbls. mayonnaise

Mix all the ingredients together and serve in individual stemmed glasses or on one large serving plate.

"Grandma, can we make some cakes?"

"Grandma, can we make some cakes?"

"Grandma, can we make some cakes?"

Although, as yet, we do not have grandchildren, I know from my sisters and friends how their grandchildren love helping in the kitchen and especially making cakes – it is often something their Mother's no longer have time to do but when visiting Grandma time passes quickly when little fingers set to work on the flour and fat! The concentration is a joy to behold even though the tasting is often something else!

As a cook, I can think of no better way of bonding with children, whether as a parent or a grandparent, than introducing them to cooking. Here are just a few ideas I have about food for toddlers and young children.

Introduce them to new flavours gradually. Present their food in small portions and they will often eat more than if they were given one single large amount.

Children are attracted by shapes and colours. Introduce these as often as you can, perhaps in the form of a garnish on tea-time sandwiches which can be decorated with small pieces of raw carrot, salad or fruit.

Remember that you are setting their eating pattern for life and the more quickly and easily they accept good wholesome food the more healthy they will become in adult life.

My children started the day with a teaspoon of cod liver oil and ended it with a mug of milky cocoa. This is doubtless considered old fashioned now, but they grew up strong and healthy and rarely missed school through illness.

The selection of recipes I give in this section will provide fun and excitement for all.

Guidelines appropriate to this section

Because these recipes are intended to be made with the help of children, I have in most cases recommended a more traditional method of mixing the ingredients together in a bowl with a wooden spoon, but as will be seen from the Lazy Cook tips, they can be mixed more quickly using a food processor.

Keep knives and sharp and hot implements away from little fingers

Always turn saucepan handles towards the centre of the hob – I find this a good practice at all times.

Ask parents if the children have any special dietary requirements, allergies, immunities etc.

Savoury, and many more recipes suitable for toddlers and children, can be found in the Main Index (beginning on page 184).

"Grandma, can we make some cakes?"

Biscuits

Easter Bonnets

     1 pkt. round Rich Tea biscuits
     1 pkt. marshmallows
     1 pkt. royal or fondant icing
     food colourings
     icing writing pencils
     iced cake decorations

Put a marshmallow in the centre of each biscuit and cover, including the biscuit, with icing. Allow to dry then decorate using icing pencils and iced cake decorations.

Lazy Cook tips – *colour the icing to make hats of different colours. Royal and ready-made fondant icings are available from cake decorating shops and supermarkets. A lovely confection to make for Easter – put one at each place setting at an Easter lunch table.*

Flapjack

     100g (4oz) butter
     25g (1oz) demerara sugar
     2 tbls. golden syrup
     225g (8oz) oats – porridge or jumbo
     50g (2oz) currants – *optional*

Set oven at gas 4/180°C/160°C fan/Aga baking oven, 3rd runner down.

Lightly oil a swiss roll tin. Melt the butter, sugar and golden syrup over a gentle heat in a large pan, stirring occasionally. Stir in the oats and fruit then spread into the prepared tin and bake for 20mins. in the pre-set oven. Remove from oven and cut into squares, allow to cool before removing from tin. Store in an airtight tin.

Lazy Cook tips – *I use jumbo oats but if making these for young children porridge oats result in a finer texture. Currants have a good nutritional value.*

Honey Oat Biscuits – *makes approx 24*

> 75g (3oz) oatmeal (or porridge oats)
> 75g (3oz) plain flour
> 1 teas. baking powder
> 50g (2oz) margarine – melted
> 1 good tbls. runny honey dissolved in 1 tbls. warm water

Set oven at gas 4/180°C/160°C fan/Aga baking oven, 3rd runner down.

Lightly oil or grease a large baking tray. Putting all ingredients into a bowl and mix together with a wooden spoon until a paste is formed (gather together by hand). Place small amounts (approx. large teaspoon size) on to the prepared baking tray, flatten with a wet fork and bake in the pre-set oven for 20mins. or until beginning to turn a biscuit colour. Remove from oven and cool on a wire tray. Store in an airtight container.

Lazy Cook tips – *the cooked biscuits will be of a smoother texture if oatmeal is used. Can be mixed in a food processor (please read* **Guidelines** *on page 42). Shape and bake as intructed above or in the method described in Oatmeal Biscuits on page 45.*

Iced Biscuits

Spread Rich Tea or Marie biscuits with water icing (recipe on page 52). Dip into chopped nuts, raisins or grated chocolate and leave to set. If making for a party write each child's name on the iced biscuits using Writing Icing sticks available from specialist icing shops and supermarkets.

Oatmeal Biscuits – *makes approx. 24*

> 75g (3oz) porridge oats
> 75g (3oz) plain flour
> 1/2 teas. baking powder
> 1 teas. sugar – *optional*
> 50g (2oz) margarine – softened
> 2 good tbls. warm water

Make as directed in recipe for Honey Oat Biscuits on page 44, but you might like to follow my alternative method of rolling and shaping as follows:

Put the paste on to a lightly floured board and shape into a ball. Put this on to the prepared baking tray and roll it out to approx. 3mm (1/8″) thickness. Cut into squares of the size required (including the ragged ends) and bake in the pre-set oven for 15–20mins. or until turning to a light biscuit colour. Allow to cool before breaking along the cut lines. Store in an airtight tin.

Lazy Cook tips *– this method of rolling and shaping the biscuits is quick and gives the finished biscuits a nice home-made appearance. Can be made using wholemeal flour when an extra tablespoon of water will be needed.*

Rusks

Cut a wholemeal or white loaf into 2.5cm (1″) thick slices and cut each slice into fingers not less than 5cm (2″) long. Place them on a baking tray and leave in a warm oven gas 2/150°C/130°C fan/Aga simmering oven) until crisp throughout. When cold store in an airtight tin.

Lazy Cook tips – *serve only to toddlers who can digest and chew solid food.*

"Grandma, can we make some cakes?"

Buns

Chocolate and Banana Buns – *makes 12*

Children will enjoy making these not least because the end product is so good to eat! Can also be made for adults using crystallised or stem ginger pieces in place of chocolate.

> 100g (4oz) margarine – softened
> 75g (3oz) brown sugar
> 100g (4oz) plain flour
> 1 heaped teas. baking powder
> 2 large eggs – whisk together
> 1 large banana
> 100g (4oz) chocolate chips – milk or plain
> paper cases

Set oven at gas 4/180°C/160°C fan/Aga baking oven, 3rd runner down. Put the paper cases into a 12 hole patti tin.

Put the softened margarine and sugar into a large mixing bowl and mix together using a wooden spoon. Add the flour, baking powder and eggs and mix until smooth. Add the chocolate chips and the peeled banana cut into thick slices directly into the bowl. Stir all together then spoon into the paper cases and bake in the pre-set oven for 20–30mins. or until browning and firm to the touch in the centre. Remove from oven and cool on a wire tray. Store in an airtight tin, eat within 2 days.

Lazy Cook tips – *the texture of the cooked buns should be lumpy with banana pieces and streaky with chocolate. Can be mixed in a food processor (please read **Guidelines** on page 42). Bake as directed in the recipe.*

Currant Buns *– makes approx 12*

225g (8oz) plain flour
2 teas. baking powder
50g (2oz) caster sugar
50g (2oz) margarine – softened
2 tbls. milk
1 large egg
100g (4oz) currants

Set oven at gas 4/180°C/350°F/Aga baking oven, 3rd runner down.
Drop small cake liners into a 12 hole patti tin.

Put all the ingredients into a bowl and mix to a smooth consistency
with a wooden spoon. Spoon into the cake liners and bake in the pre-
set oven for 15–20mins. or until they rise and brown slightly and are
firm to the touch in the centre. Remove from oven and cool on a
wire tray. Store in an airtight container and use within 5 days or
freeze.

Lazy Cook tips *– if the mixture is too firm add a little more milk to soften.
Can be mixed in a food processor (please read* **Guidelines** *on page 42).
Shape and bake as directed in the recipe.*

Hot X Buns *– makes 12*

Children love handling and shaping dough mixtures.

450g (1lb) strong plain flour
2 teas. mixed spice
50g (2oz) caster sugar
50g (2oz) margarine or lard
50g (2oz) currants or sultanas
25g (1oz) fresh yeast
2 large eggs
milk – approx 300ml (10fl.oz)

Crumble the yeast into a measuring jug and mix to a smooth paste
with a little cold milk. Whisk in the eggs and make it up to 300ml

"Grandma, can we make some cakes?"

(10fl.oz) with milk. Mix the flour, spice and sugar together in a large bowl, rub in the chosen fat, then mix in the fruit. Make a well in the centre, pour in the yeast mixture and work together into a ball of dough. Remove from bowl and knead on a lightly floured surface until the dough is smooth. Cut into 12 pieces and shape each into a ball. Place on a lightly oiled baking tray, flatten with the palm of your hand and then mark with a cross using a blunt knife. Put in a warm place to rise (at this point set the oven to gas 7/220°C/200°C fan/Aga roasting oven, 2nd runner down). When the buns have doubled in size bake in the pre-set oven for 15–20mins. reducing the temperature after 10mins. to gas 4/180°C/160°C fan/Aga baking oven. Cool on a wire tray. Serve warm, split and spread with butter or a spread of your choice. Will freeze.

Lazy Cook tips – *my method for these buns, as with all home bread making is "shape – rise – bake". They can also be mixed very quickly in a food processor (see below). Strong plain flour should always be used for bread making. Dried yeast can be used, follow the instructions on the packet. Fresh yeast can be frozen, freeze in 25g (1oz) packets. The warmth of the kitchen should be sufficient to rise the dough, it will even rise if put into a polythene bag and placed in a refrigerator – the longer the dough takes to rise, the better the texture of the bread. For many years we have invited friends in to Coffee and Hot X Buns on the morning of Good Friday. Such an event is also an easy way of fund-raising for your church.*

To mix in a food processor – *process the flour, spice and sugar for a few seconds. Add the fruit and process again pouring the yeast and milk mixture through the funnel until a ball of dough is formed. Continue shaping and baking as directed in the recipe.*

Cakes

Humpty-Dumpty cake – an Easter cake to delight children
of all ages

I suggest the cake is made before the children come on to the scene
and they can enjoy decorating it.

For the cake
225g (8oz) margarine – softened
225g (8oz) self-raising flour
175g (6oz) caster sugar
3 large eggs
2 tbls milk

For the decoration
900g (2lb) ready-made fondant icing
apricot jam
food colouring – of your own choice
1 large hollow Easter egg
a variety of smaller Easter eggs, some in foil wrappings
1 cake board, or foil covered tray

To make the cake

Set oven at gas 4/180°C/160°C fan/Aga baking oven, 3rd runner
down. Line the base and ends of a 900gm (2lb) loaf tin with
greaseproof paper and oil lightly.

Put the flour and sugar into a food processor and process for a few
seconds before adding the softened margarine, eggs, and milk and
process for a few seconds until
smooth. Pour into the
prepared tin, smooth the top
and bake in the pre-set oven
for 40–45mins. or until set
(test with a metal skewer).
Cool a little before removing
from the tin on to a wire tray.

"Grandma, can we make some cakes?"

To decorate

Place the cake on a board or tray before spreading all over lightly with jam then cover with rolled fondant. Colour some of the fondant, roll, cut into strips, brush lightly with water and place round the sides of the cake to represent a wall. Using a warm knife cut the base from the large hollow egg and sit the remaining egg on the top of the cake (cut side down), secure with a little melted chocolate or jam. Use more coloured fondant to shape into legs and place them dangling down the cake from the egg (secure with a brushing of water). Using more coloured fondant, (or an icing writing stick), put a face and hair on the egg, also on some of the smaller eggs and place these around and on the cake.

Lazy Cook tips – *the cake can be mixed in a large bowl using an electric hand whisk or wooden spoon or if you prefer, buy a ready-made cake of the shape required. Cut the decorations from Fondant, or use Icing Writing Sticks. Children will have great fun helping to decorate the cake. To make into an Easter birthday cake add the appropriate number of candles.*

Mock Custard Creams – *makes approx. 6*

600ml (1pt) thick Bird's custard
12 cream crackers
few spots vanilla extract
water icing – recipe on page 52

Make the custard to a thick consistency, flavour with vanilla extract and leave in the saucepan until cold. Sandwich pairs of crackers together with a thick layer of custard (approx. 5mm/$^1/_2$″), until all the custard has been used. Spread the tops with water icing and allow to set before serving.

Lazy Cook tips – *cover the made custard with a plate or piece of wet greaseproof paper to prevent a skin forming. Do not over-sweeten the custard, I recommend one dessertspoon sugar then test for sweetness The custard and icing softens the crackers. As a child I remember my elder sister making these and I loved them, they were our version of Vanilla Slices made with puff or flaky pastry.*

Water icing

Sieve 225g (8oz) icing sugar into a bowl, make a well in the centre and pour in cold water, a little at a time, until a spreadable consistency is formed. Dip a knife blade into warm water to make the spreading of the icing easier. Colour with food colouring if wished.

Rock Cakes – *makes 10–12*

225g (8oz) plain flour
2 teas. baking powder
75g. (3oz) demerara sugar
1/2 teas. mixed spice
50g (2oz) margarine
25g (1oz) lard
1 large egg
1 tbls. milk
100g (4oz) currants or sultanas
little runny honey – *optional*

Set oven at gas 4/180°C/160°C fan/Aga baking oven, 3rd runner down.

Lightly oil a baking tray. Put the flour and baking powder into a large bowl, add the fats and rub in until a breadcrumb texture. Add the remaining ingredients (except the honey) and mix to a sticky paste. Using two forks pile into rocky heaps on to the prepared baking tray and bake for 10–15mins. or until brown and crisp. Put on a wire tray and pour a little runny honey on to each hot cake (optional). Eat when cool.

Lazy Cook tips – *can be mixed in a food processor (please read **Guidelines** on page 42). Shape and bake as directed in the recipe. Best eaten the day they are made.*

"Grandma, can we make some cakes?"

Train Cake

    2 chocolate Swiss rolls
    1 pkt. Liquorice Allsorts – *optional*
    1 large packet Smarties Chocolate Beans
    4 chocolate finger biscuits
    little chocolate butter cream – recipe below
    6 chocolate digestive biscuits
    candles – the appropriate number
    long chopping board or tray covered with foil

Assemble directly on to the covered board or tray.

To make the engine, cut the first roll into two cutting one piece slightly longer. Stand the shorter half on it's end and stick it to the longer half with butter cream. Decorate the front to resemble a face using Liquorice Allsorts, or Writing Icing Sticks. To make the wagons, cut the second roll into two even lengths. Cut out a little of the cake from the top of each to form a cavity and fill each with Smarties. Link these to each other and to the engine with chocolate finger biscuits. Using the butter cream stick Smarties round the edge of each of the digestive biscuits and stick one of these to each side of the engine and wagons to resemble the wheels. Place the appropriate number of candles into the top of the engine to resemble chimneys – and it is ready for serving! Sketch on page 73.

Chocolate butter cream

    50g (2oz) softened butter or margarine
    100g (4oz) icing sugar
    1 teas. cocoa powder or drinking chocolate

Blend all ingredients together until smooth and add a little milk if necessary to form a soft spreadable consistency. Increase the quantities to make a larger amount. Will keep for 4–5 days in a covered container in a refrigerator.

Chocolates

Chocolate Discs – *makes approx 30*

> 225g (8oz) chocolate – milk, white or bitter
> toppings – listed below

Melt the chocolate then drop from a teaspoon on to foil. Leave to set or top with an ingredient or your choice. When set peel from the foil or store (on the foil), in a box.

Topping suggestions

> hundreds and thousands
> dried fruit
> a Smartie (or any individual small chocolate or sweet)
> nuts – whole or chopped – check dietary requirements
> crystallized ginger pieces (for older children and adults)

Marshmallow/Valentine Chocolates

> 1 pkt. marshmallows
> 100g (4oz) milk or bitter chocolate
> sugar or silver hearts – *optional*

Warm the chocolate in a basin until it has melted. Drop the marshmallows into the chocolate one at a time and coat. Remove with a fork and place on foil. Peel from foil when set and serve or store in a box.

Lazy Cook tips *– use a fork to lift the marshmallows from the chocolate. These make excellent Valentine chocolates if topped with a sugar or silver heart before the chocolate has set.*

Serving Suggestions *– I like to put these into the refrigerator and serve them cold. They can be put into individual chocolate cases and packed into boxes or pretty bags to give as gifts. Children enjoy making them for parents and friends.*

"Grandma, can we make some cakes?"

Puddings

Banana Custard – *serves 4–6*

4–6 bananas
600ml (1pt) full cream milk
2 desst. Birds custard powder
1 tbsp. granulated sugar
few drops vanilla extract – *optional*
284ml (10fl.oz) whipping, or thick single cream – *optional*
1 tbls. grated chocolate

Half fill a serving, or trifle dish with peeled, sliced bananas. Mix the custard powder to a smooth paste using a little of the cold milk. Warm the remaining milk, add the custard powder paste, vanilla essence and sugar and stir until it boils and thickens, remove from heat and allow to cool a little before pouring over the bananas. Serve when the custard is set and cold with, or without the cream spread on top and scattered with grated chocolate.

Lazy Cook tips – *make in individual glasses or dishes if you prefer. I recommend you keep in store a tin of Charbonnel et Walker Chocolate Charbonnel – much quicker than grating chocolate.*

Serving Suggestions – *a real comfort food loved by children and adults alike.*

Chocolate and Banana Butties

For each butty
2 rounds bread
butter
chocolate – pieces, buttons or chips
banana slices

Butter each bread slice and sandwich together with chocolate pieces and banana slices. Toast on each side.

Lazy Cook tips – *children love these. Toast on a lightly oiled hob, under a grill, in a sandwich toaster or in an Aga toasting rack. Make for older children and adults using ginger pieces in place of chocolate and scatter a little powdered ginger on the bread before assembling into a sandwich.*

Chocolate Blancmange

> 600ml (1pt) full cream milk
> 2 rounded desst. cornflour
> 1 rounded desst. cocoa powder (or drinking chocolate)
> 1 level tbls. granulated sugar

Mix the cornflour, cocoa powder and sugar together with a little of the milk. Bring the remaining milk to a simmer, add the cornflour mixture and bring to boil over a gentle heat, stirring continuously with a wooden spoon or spatula. Taste for sweetness before pouring into a mould which has been dampened with cold water. Leave in a fridge or cold larder to set. To unmould, loosen the sides using fingertips and shake the blancmange on to a serving plate.

Lazy Cook tips – *animal shaped moulds are fun to use when making chocolate blancmange for children. If drinking chocolate is used a little less sugar can be added.*

Fresh Orange Jelly

> 300ml (½pt) hot water
> 1 tbls. runny honey
> 25g (1oz) gelatine crystals
> 4 oranges – squeezed
> 1 lemon – squeezed

"Grandma, can we make some cakes?"

Stir the gelatine crystals and honey into the hot water until dissolved then leave until cold before stirring in the fruit juices. Taste for sweetness and add more honey or a little brown sugar if needed. Pour into one large or several small jelly moulds or ramekins and put into a refrigerator or cold larder until set.

Lazy Cook tips – *serve direct from the dish/es or unmould by loosening the jelly from the side of the mould using fingertips and shake it on to a serving dish. Alternatively, stand the mould in very hot water for a few seconds then shake the jelly on to a serving plate.*

Serving Suggestions – *with sponge drops, ice cream or single cream.*

Fruit Purée

Lazy Cook tips – *when making for toddlers and young children. fruit with pips and seeds should be rubbed through a sieve once cooked. Remove the skin and stones of large fruits, apples, pears, peaches, nectarines, apricots, plums, etc. Cook in bulk and freeze in individual helpings. Sweeten to taste with runny honey or raw cane sugar. Cook the fruit in a little water until it is soft and liquidise or process to a purée before serving to toddlers and young children. When cold store, covered, in a fridge and use within 3 days. To freeze, pack the cold purée into freezer bags of varying sizes, label and date.*

Apple
One of the easiest and most successful purée.

Peel, core and slice bramley apples into a pan with just enough water to moisten the base. Add several whole cloves (optional), place lid on pan and cook over a gentle heat until the apples pulp and rise in the pan, remove from heat. Follow instructions for sweetening, storing or freezing in Lazy Cook tips above.

Pear

Peel and discard the skin. Cut into quarters and remove centre core and pips. Follow instructions for cooking, sweetening, storing or freezing in Lazy Cook tips on page 57.

Peach, Nectarine, Apricot, Plum

Wash the whole fruit before cutting in half and removing and discarding the stones. Slice or quarter and follow instructions for cooking, sweetening, storing or freezing in Lazy Cook tips on page 57.

Rhubarb

When the rhubarb is young there should be no need to remove the outer skin. Wash, top and tail each stick and cut into lengths approx. 2cm/1″ lengths. Follow instructions for cooking, sweetening, storing or freezing in Lazy Cook tips on page 57.

"Grandma, can we make some cakes?"

Let's Party

Recipes and Menu suggestions for Lazy Cook entertaining

The most informal country garden is often the one into which the most thought has been given and this is so with entertaining. Give thought, not merely to the menu, but to the overall comfort of your guests, keep the food simple and the occasion will be relaxed and informal – just as planned!

Guidelines appropriate to this section

Drinks Parties

Savouries to be passed around with drinks should be mouthsized, plentiful and varying in flavour. Towards the end of the party offer a small selection of sweetmeats. These can be in the form of mini biscuits or pastries and chocolates (bought or homemade). Include also seedless grapes or small orange segments.

Offer cocktail sticks where appropriate, I put these in egg cups.

Do not overcrowd ingredients on to too small a plate.

Supper and Dinner Parties

When planning these think of the meal as a whole. Include a variety of colours, textures and flavours. Avoid repeating any particular ingredient in more than one course, eg. if mushrooms form part of the starter, to not include them in the main course.

Keep it simple – too many flavours will confuse the palate.

Avoid using untested/untried recipes.

Large parties

Do as much *advanced preparation* as possible including getting extra china, cutlery and serving dishes out of cupboards. Remember to buy serviettes, or check that linen napkins are in a pristine condition if these are to be used. Set table/s.

Menu

You want to look relaxed and good when your guests arrive so keep the food simple. Avoid recipes which will cause stress by needing too much last minute preparation, garnish or decoration – remember the most simple presentation is often the most eye-catching.

Drinks

Has your partner remembered to get these, and hire extra glasses!

Washing-up

Pay for it to be done.

Canapés for a drinks party

In addition to a selection of nuts, crisps and other bought savouries which often come under the heading "nibbles" and are easy to hand around with the first drink, there is nothing more inviting than the aroma of baking as you enter a house. Some of the recipes I recommend in this section can be prepared in advance or baked just before your guests arrive, or even during the party and I promise they will make your parties the talk of the town. Most of these recipes are made using store-cupboard ingredients and some can be prepared the night before in readiness to pop into the oven to bake at a time to suit you – very quick, very delicious, very relaxing, very Lazy Cook.

Cherubs on Horseback

> several packets of lean, rindless, streaky bacon
> dried apricot halves

Pre-set oven gas 6/200°C/180°C fan/Aga roasting oven, 2nd runner down.

Stretch each bacon rasher by stroking it with a knife then cut it in half. To each half add a dried apricot half, roll up and thread on to metal skewers. Place on a swiss roll or similar baking tin and cook in a pre-set oven, or under a grill for 10–15mins. or until the bacon is cooked – turn halfway through cooking. Remove from the skewers on to kitchen roll to absorb all excess fat, and serve hot.

Lazy Cook tips *– these can be prepared many hours before the party in readiness for cooking. To serve pierce each with a cocktail stick or put a pot of cocktail sticks on the serving dish for guests to use if they wish. These can also be served as a starter by popping a few on to individual salads. A refreshing change from the more familiar 'Angels' and 'Devils' on horseback.*

Ham and Walnut Bites *– makes approx. 36*

4 thick bread slices
100g (4oz) cooked ham
50g (2oz) butter – softened
2 teas. creamed horseradish
2 teas. Dijon mustard
2 teas. cranberry sauce
1 small onion – skin and finely chop
75g (3oz) shelled walnuts – halves or pieces

Break the bread into a food processor and process until crumbed, remove half and keep for coating. Put all remaining ingredients into the processor and process until a paste is formed. Drop from a spoon into the reserved breadcrumbs and shape in the palm of your hands into rounds – serve with drinks or cocktails.

Lazy Cook tips *– if the processed mixture is too dry, add a little oil or cream. These can be made 3–4 days before the party and stored in a sealed container in a fridge or cold larder. Bring back to room temperature before serving*

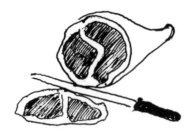

Savoury Bacon Dumplings – *makes approx. 20*

Parsley and Thyme Forcemeat – recipe on page 25
20 rashers rindless streaky bacon

Set oven at gas 6/200°C/180°C fan/Aga roasting oven, 2nd runner down.

Stretch each bacon rasher by stroking it with a knife. Cut in half and place together like a cross. Put a good teaspoon of the forcemeat at the point where the slices cross and cover with the bacon ends to make into a parcel. Put into a shallow baking tin, bacon ends down, and cook in the pre-set oven for 10-15mins. or until the bacon is cooked. Serve hot, warm or cold.

Lazy Cook tips – *in addition to serving these at a party they are excellent served with meat and fish recipes. Make in sizes to suit your requirements. Can be made in advance of cooking and can be stored when cooked, covered, in a refrigerator or cold larder. Use within 5 days.*

Savoury Sticks – *makes 30–40*

1 pkt. ready-rolled puff pastry
Choice of toppings
sun-dried tomato paste
tapenade
pesto
curry paste
grated parmesan or Stilton
mixed herbs

Set oven at gas 6/200°C/180°C fan/Aga roasting oven, 2nd runner down.

Roll a sheet of ready-rolled puff pastry on a lightly floured board or surface until it is double in size and place this on a baking tray.

Spread with one of the above toppings and cut into strips not less than 1cm x 5cm (½" x 2"). Bake in the pre-set oven for 10–15mins. or until the pastry has risen. Break into the cut strips and drain on kitchen roll. Serve hot.

Lazy Cook tips – *cut the re-rolled pastry to fit the size of your baking sheet/s. If topping with cheese or herbs you will need to brush the pastry with milk or beaten egg before adding these ingredients. The cuts made before baking may have closed up during baking, re-cut with a sharp knife or scissors. These sticks can be prepared many hours before they are baked, I have often prepared them the day before and baked them during the party. I recommend you keep a packet of ready rolled puff pastry in the freezer. Make lots, they will be popular.*

Shortcrust Bases with Savoury Toppings
– makes approx 40 x 2.5cm/1" squares

225g/8oz shortcrust pastry – bought or home-made (page 65)
Suggested toppings
meat pâté topped with a red or white seedless grape
mackerel or salmon pâté topped with a prawn
cream cheese seasoned with chopped parsley and topped with a
    piece of radish
cream cheese topped with a curl of smoked salmon or Parma ham

To shape and bake the pastry bases
Set oven at gas 6/200°C/180°C fan/Aga roasting oven, 2nd runner down.

Roll the pastry out to approx. 5mm/¼" thickness on a lightly floured surface, to as near a square or rectangle as you can then place it on a lightly oiled baking tray. Prick it all over with a fork before marking into squares of the size required. Bake in the pre-set oven for 10–15mins. or until the pastry begins to change colour. Remove from oven and snap or cut along the marked squares to separate. Use immediately or allow to cool before storing in an airtight tin or container until required.

Lazy Cook tips – *this method of shaping the bases is much quicker than using pastry cutters and transferring them one by one on to a baking tray. When serving at a drinks party mouthsized bases should be cut. Can also be made using wholemeal pastry.*

Shortcrust or Wholemeal Pastry

100g (4oz) plain white flour
100g (4oz) wholemeal flour
100g (4oz) lard
50–75ml (2–3 fl.oz) cold water

Set oven at gas 6/200°C/180°C fan/Aga roasting oven, 2nd runner down.

Put the flours into a food processor and process for a few seconds. Add the lard in pieces and process for a few seconds before pouring the liquid through the funnel until a ball of pastry is formed, switch off. Remove the pastry from the processor, shape into a ball and roll to the thickness required, on a lightly floured board.

Lazy Cook tips – *for shortcrust pastry use all white flour. We are often advised on the importance of allowing the pastry to rest in a refrigerator before baking. On the very few occasions I have attempted this I have forgotten it and ended up trying to roll rock hard pastry. "Keep it Simple" is my motto "make – roll – bake" then relax in anticipation of the meal!*

Toad in the Hole – recipe on page 122

"A Cook's Nightmare"

The arrangements for our dinner party had gone well. We hadn't entertained for a long time and ten friends had been invited for 7.30p.m.

I had already cooked the main course which was resting in the refrigerator in readiness for reheating. Making a fruit salad for pudding, setting the table and arranging a floral centrepiece had somehow taken up most of the morning. There just remained the vegetables and the starter to prepare – time to take a break. It was 5-o-clock, not too soon I decided to make the Salmon Parcels and put one at each serving place. They took a little longer than I had allowed but they looked nice and would be a good start to what I felt was going to be a really jolly party.

My next job was to prepare the vegetables. Oh dear, I had no potatoes, how could I have overlooked buying them. The village shop will be closed, I will have to drive into Stroud. As I was leaving the family arrived home from a shopping trip to Cheltenham, they were starving as always. In my haste to reach the shops I shouted from the car, "your suppers in the fridge, you can eat it all".

Halfway to Stroud and it dawned on me that if the village shop was closed all the town shops would be also. I did a U turn and decided to serve rice in place of potatoes – I think I have some rice!!!!! As I entered the house something told me to look in the dining room, oh no, I was just in time to see Silver our cat finish off the last of the salmon parcels, she looked bloated and eager for the door. I had been so careful to lock her outside, she must have sneaked in with the family who appeared, all smiles, "thanks for the supper. It was delicious but we had a job to finish it all!". After a moment of confusion something told me to look in the fridge, oh no, they had eaten the supper I had prepared for my dinner party. What was I to do? No starter, no potatoes and now no main course. I glanced at the clock it was 7.35p.m. any minute now our friends would arrive, there was no food and I was in no fit state to receive them – at that very moment there was a ringing in my ears, it was the alarm clock – never was I more pleased to be woken – I shot out of bed, there was much to do if everying was to be ready for the party tonight.

Menu suggestions for entertaining

Picnic in the Park

Plays and concerts performed in the park or in the grounds of a country house have become a part of the English summer scene and this is made even more enjoyable if it starts with a picnic. The recipes I recommend as well as being quick to prepare, can be packed and transported easily – they can be presented on a platter, or plated straight from plastic containers – whichever way, I can promise you they will taste delicious and the picnic will be as memorable as the entertainment.

Menu

Antipasto of roasted vegetables and Rosemary selection of Bread or Rolls

✸

Platter of Smoked Salmon Rolls, Parma Ham, Roll Mop Herrings and Egg Halves topped with Anchovies, all garnished with a few Fresh Strawberries

Mixed Salad
Vinaigrette
Grain Mustard

✸

Sacher Torte with Whipped Cream and Chocolate Truffles

✸

Coffee

Cool Drinks and Hot Dogs for a last minute Summer Party

Catch the moment – so often elaborate parties are planned and suddenly those warm summer days and evenings turn to cloud and there is disappointment. This menu is perfect for last minute entertaining when all can share in the cooking and the enjoyment – everything is easy – my kind of entertaining.

Menu

Chilled Rosé
Soft drinks

❋

Hot Dogs

❋

Fresh Fruit Meringues

❋

Cheese board

Last minute Christmas Party

Menu

Turkey Curry

❄

Baked Christmas Pudding

❄

Cheeseboard

❄

Coffee
Ginger Chocolate Discs

Summer Celebration Buffet Lunch

Menu

A selection of Canapes

❋

Simmering of Meats
Medley of Summer Vegetables
Mixed Green Salad
Tomato and Basil Salad
New Potatoes dressed with Olive Oil and Chopped Chives
Mayonnaise
Vinaigrette

❋

Fresh Strawberry Sponge

❋

Cheese Board

❋

Coffee
Chocolate Discs

Winter Celebration Lunch

Menu

Celeriac and Sweet Potato Soup
A selection of Breads and Rolls

Puffed up Chicken served with a Tapenade Sauce
Floret Bake
Mashed Potato

Fresh Pineapple rings with a Honey and Brandy Juice
Single Cream

Cheeseboard

Coffee
Marshmallow Chocolates

Children's Birthday Party

Fairy bells are ringing tonight
ringing in fairyland
off we go on tip-a-tip-toe
when glowworms shed their light
hark at the bells ding-dong
little ones come along
there's going to be a fairy wedding
in fairyland tonight

My late aunt Edie used to sing this to me. She remembered being taught it as a little girl at dancing classes – it still captures the attention and enchants small children.

Menu

Gangplank
Cheese Fingers
Shortcrust Pastry Bases with Savoury Toppings
Cherubs on Horseback
Raw Carrot and Celery Sticks

Fresh Orange Jelly decorated with Fresh Fruit Slices
Ice Cream
Banana Custard

Iced Biscuits
Petit Meringues

Train Cake

Menu suggestions for entertaining

I remember our own children's birthday parties well and although they were very different from those of today they were, nonetheless, very happy times.

Held at home, they began with indoor and outdoor games and quizzes. The birthday tea was easily stretched until going home time. The children were all seated around the dining table, crackers were pulled, paper hats put on then we all joined in attempting to guess the answers to the mottoes.

Tea was served in separate courses between which I would recite a short rhyme or tell a short story, (*The Owl and the Pussycat*, or similar), or lead them in a traditional song, preferably with accompanying actions. Any child who was keen and able was invited to perform their own party piece. The birthday cake and blowing out of the candles was the highlight of the tea. Before leaving, each child picked from a bag of 'lucky dips' which consisted of small bags, tubes or bars of sweets or chocolate, each individually wrapped – happy memories.

Light Meals –
Snacks – Starters

All in one breakfast/brunch

– when catering for a crowd

>*For each serving*
>1 tbls. oil
>1 slice bread
>1 large mushroom
>1 egg
>1 small tomato
>pinch sugar
>2 rashers back bacon or 4 lean streaky rashers

Set oven at gas 6/200°C/180°C fan/Aga roasting oven, top runner.

Heat the oil in a roasting tin, dip in the bread and leave dipped side down. Remove the stalk from the mushroom, put the whole mushroom on the bread and the stalk in the tin. Crack an egg in to the mushroom cavity, top with slices of tomato and sprinkle with a pinch of sugar. Drape with the bacon slices and put into the pre-set oven and cook for 10–15mins. or until the bacon has cooked. Serve immediately.

Lazy Cook tips *– the choice of mushroom is important, select ones with the suggestion of a cavity or with a thick peel which will contain the egg. Should the white trickle from the mushroom on to the toast and beyond, this doesn't matter but it is best if the yolk is not broken. An excellent way of serving breakfast or brunch to a crowd. Both sides of the bread can be oiled if you wish.*

Serving Suggestions *– straight from the oven with Tomato Ketchup or HP sauce.*

Beef Tomatoes with a Savoury Filling

– makes 4

    4 beef tomatoes
    4 heaped tablespoons breadcrumbs
    4 spring onions – thinly sliced
    12–16 anchovy fillets – cut into small pieces
    fresh mint – roughly chopped
    freshly ground black pepper
    2 teas. runny honey
    a little oil or butter

Set oven at gas 6/200°C/180°C fan/Aga roasting oven, 3rd runner down.

Slice the top (stalk end) from the tomatoes and keep. Remove the pips and centre core and put these into a sieve placed over a basin to drain off and collect all the juices. Prepare the onions, anchovies and mint and add these to the tomato juices with the breadcrumbs and freshly ground pepper and stir together. Pack this into the prepared tomatoes and pour ½ teas. runny honey on top, cover with the reserved tops. Lightly oil a shallow ovenproof dish, add the tomatoes and lightly oil these all over before baking in the pre-set oven for 15–20mins. or until baked. Serve hot, warm or cold.

Lazy Cook tips – use a grapefruit knife to remove the centre core and pips from the tomatoes. The filling should be of a moist consistency, add a little stock or warm water if too dry. Make breadcrumbs in a blender or processer or use dried breadcrumbs (recipe on page 151). Can be cooked on a barbecue, wrap them individually in foil before cooking.

Serving Suggestions *– with salad for a delicious light lunch. If serving as a starter use smaller tomatoes. Serve also as a vegetable accompaniment with cooked meat or fish.*

Fish in Batter – recipe on page 26

Fresh Figs in little Bread Baskets

To make 1
1 fresh fig
1 rasher back bacon
a little made English mustard
1 bread roll – brown or white
a little oil

Set oven at gas 6/200°C/180°C fan/Aga roasting oven, 3rd runner down.

Wrap the fig in the bacon rasher (like a jacket), and stand it in a lightly oiled shallow ovenproof dish and bake, uncovered, for 8–10mins. or until the bacon is cooked. Cut the top from the roll and scoop out the centre to form a cavity, butter or oil, put on a baking tray and bake until brown and crisp (4–5mins). Remove from oven and spread a little made mustard on the base before putting a baked fig inside. Pour any pan juices over the fig.

Lazy Cook tips *– this is a good combination of sweet and savoury flavours. Secure the bacon ends with a wooden cocktail stick (avoid piercing the fig), or, if baking several, place them close together in the dish with the loose bacon ends touching, and this will prevent the bacon unwrapping during cooking. Make the unused bread into breadcrumbs. Serve as a starter or light meal with a watercress garnish. When the fig is cut into the juices escape and flavour and moisten the bread basket.*

Gangplank – *to feed a gang*

This is another idea passed on to me by Evy, my Norweigan relative, a wonderful cook and hostess and one of my favourite people.

> 1 French Stick/Baguette or Ciabatta loaf
> 100–175g (4–6oz) cream cheese
> freshly chopped parsley
> freshly ground white pepper
> several slices each, smoked salmon and Black Forest or Parma ham
> 2 eggs – boil, peel and slice
> cocktail gherkins
> pitted olives
> seedless grapes or strawberry quarters if in season
> box of cress

Slice the top from the loaf and tear the bread from the base to form a cavity. Mix the parsley into the cheese then spread it thickly over the base of the cavity. Top with the remaining ingredients, shredding the salmon and ham slices, and finally scatter with the cress. Cut into chunks to serve with mixed salad, vinaigrette and mayonnaise.

Lazy Cook tips – this is the Lazy Cook alternative to making lots of sandwiches. The finished loaf is colourful and eye-catching in presentation and tastes good. Children will enjoy making it. The amount and the choice of fillings is yours and will be dependent on whether you are feeding adults or children. In summer many salad ingredients can be included to add flavour and texture. Both halves of a loaf can be filled Any remaining bread can be made into breadcrumbs, dried and stored for future use. Recipes for home-made vinaigrette and mayonnaise can be found on pages 86 and 32. A Ciabatta loaf will make 4 adult servings.

Hot Dogs

> sausages
> onions
> oil
> finger rolls
> HP and Tomato Ketchup
> variety of made mustards

Barbecue, grill or bake the sausages in a roasting tin in a hot oven (gas 6/200°C/180°C fan/Aga roasting oven, 2nd runner down). Heat some oil in a large sauté or frying pan. Skin and slice the onions, add to the hot oil, put lid on pan and cook until the onions are beginning to soften. Split the bread rolls and fill with onion and a sausage. Serve on a hot plate or in a serviette.

Lazy Cook tips – *allow approximately one small onion and one sausage to each roll. Guests will choose from the sauces and mustards.*

Lazy Cheese Soufflé – *serves 4*

> 6 rounds of bread – brown or white
> 225g (8oz) grated cheese
> 425ml (15fl.oz) full cream milk
> 3 large eggs
> freshly ground white pepper
> 2 teas. Dijon mustard
> 1 teas. anchovy essence
> 4–6 anchovies – *optional*

Set oven at gas 4/180°C/160°C fan/Aga baking oven.

Layer the bread and cheese into a soufflé or pie dish (or a basin), beginning and ending with bread. Warm the milk. Whisk the eggs, add the mustard and anchovy essence and season with pepper before adding the milk and whisking together. Pour through a sieve over the layered bread and leave for 15–20mins. Place a few anchovies on top, stand the dish on a baking tray and bake in the preset oven for 30–40mins. or until well risen. Serve straight from the oven as a starter, or with peas or mangetout, or salad as a light meal.

Lazy Cook tips – *this is a good recipe for using up ends of cheese especially Stilton which will give good flavour. It can be left for a longer period before baking if it suits your time plan.*

Omelettes – basic recipe for a 1, 2 or 3 egg omelette

12g (¹/₂oz) butter
2–3 large eggs
freshly ground white pepper
filling of own choice
parsley sprigs and chives for garnish – *optional*

Lightly mix the eggs and pepper together with a fork. Heat an omelette pan before adding the butter and when it has melted and is hot add the eggs and immediately draw a wooden spatula through the eggs several times to build up layers of egg before it begins to set. Add a chosen filling, fold in half, then shake it on to a hot serving plate.

Lazy Cook tips *– omelettes are best cooked quickly over a good heat and for this reason it is essential to use a heavy-based omelette pan. To test the correct temperature of the butter before adding the egg drop a few spots of the egg from the fork into the pan and it should immediately set. Do not overwhisk the eggs before cooking, just mix the yolk and white together with a fork. Always serve direct from the pan, they will collapse and toughen as they cool in the pan. Popular fillings are fresh herbs, grated cheese, and cooked sliced mushrooms. When serving to children make using one egg only and a filling they will enjoy*

Serving Suggestions *– an enjoyable meal for lunch or supper. Serve with thin slices of buttered bread and salad.*

Melon Cups – recipe on page 37

Peach Halves Baked with a Savoury Filling

To each ripe peach you need
1 teas. grain mustard
2 thin slices goats cheese
2 slices Parma ham
watercress
radish – left whole
oil and balsamic vinegar

Set oven at gas 4/180°C/160°C fan/Aga baking oven, 2nd runner down.

Wash the peaches before cutting in half, remove and discard the stone, fill the cavities with a little grain mustard. Top with a slice of goats cheese and a crumpled slice of Parma ham. Place on a baking tray or in an ovenproof dish and bake for 5–10mins in the pre-set oven. Serve with a few sprigs of watercress topped with a whole radish and drizzled with oil and balsamic vinegar – one third vinegar to oil.

Lazy Cook tips – *cut a sliver from the base of the peaches so that they will stand firm while cooking. I recommend Mustarde de Meaux 'Pommery' grain mustard. A little hot water can be added to the dish to encourage softening of the peaches during cooking.*

Serving Suggestions – *serve hot or cold allowing one half peach per person as a starter, or two halves as a light snack with toasted brioche.*

Poached Egg with a Rocket and Parma Ham salad

To make individual servings
1 egg – poached
1 thick slice bread or brioche – toasted
butter – *optional*
rocket – wash and dry
1 pickled gherkin or cornichon – sliced
vinaigrette
1 slice Parma or similar smoked ham
freshly ground black pepper
chives

Put approx. 300ml (10fl.oz) water into a small pan with a few drops vinegar added and when boiling crack an egg into it. Reduce to a simmer, put lid on pan and simmer for 2–3mins. or until the egg is cooked to your liking. Meanwhile make and butter the toast and put on a serving plate. Cover with the prepared rocket, scatter with slices of gherkin and spoon over a little vinaigrette before topping with a slice of ham, crumpled. Top with the poached egg, season with freshly ground black pepper and garnish with a scattering of cut chives. Serve immediately.

Lazy Cook tips – *whisk the boiling water before adding the egg for an even coagulation. Watercress can be used in place of rocket. A light but substantial lunch.*

Salads

Salads are an important part of my daily diet and because I enjoy seasonal ingredients, winter salads differ in content from summer. The quantities given are approximate and serve one person. I recommend a 'salad spinner' for perfectly dried lettuce and similar salad-like ingredients.

Daily Summer Salad

> collection of mixed lettuce leaves
> land cress
> lambs lettuce
> rocket
> garden mint – several leaves – cut
> spring (or red) onion – top and tail or skin and slice
> radishes – cut in half or quarter
> tomatoes – cut into halves or quarters
> cucumber – peel then cut into chunks
> several strawberries – cut in half or quarters if large
> vinaigrette – recipe on page 86

Wash and spin dry the lettuce, cress, lambs lettuce and rocket, and tear or cut up roughly before putting directly on to a plate or into a salad bowl. Add the remaining prepared ingredients and dress with vinaigrette before serving.

Lazy Cook tips – *put the prepared ingredients into a polythene bag (excluding the vinaigrette), and add them to a lunch box. I am not sure whether it is possible to buy land cress but it is easily grown in a small garden, or in pots – the flavour is similar to watercress. Serve with cold meat, poultry, fish or cooked cold vegetables, fresh bread or rolls.*

Daily Winter Salad

watercress (a handful) – wash and dry
1 spring onion – top and tail and thinly slice
celery – wash, thinly slice across a whole celery (including
    leafy tops)
1 carrot – scrub and slice
6–8 seedless grapes (red or white) – wash
1 tbls. vinaigrette – recipe on page 86

Put all prepared ingredients directly on to a plate or into a salad bowl and dress with vinaigrette before eating. Alternatively, cut the listed ingredients into lengths, put into a polythene bag (except the vinaigrette), and include in a lunch box.

Lazy Cook tips – *optional extras: pitted olives; shredded Parma, or cooked ham; crumbled Stilton cheese; chopped walnuts, cashews or pine-nuts; cooked egg yolk – chopped; smoked salmon; prawns or other shell fish; tinned sardines, salmon or tuna; avacado slices.*

Green Salad Garnished with Ham, Strawberries and Fresh Mint

mixed salad including rocket and chopped celery
vinaigrette – recipe on page 86
thinly sliced cooked ham
fresh strawberries
fresh garden mint

Wash and spin dry the salad before piling it on to individual plates or into a large serving plate or bowl. Before serving drizzle with vinaigrette and top with the ham slices torn into strips, strawberries (cut into halves or quarters if large), and scatter with chopped mint.

Lazy Cook tips – *a delicious salad full of colour and good flavours and perfect for a light lunch on a hot summer day. If you should happen to have wild strawberries growing in the garden add these.*
Parma or other thinly sliced smoked ham is also good with this recipe.

Mixed Green Salad

    mixed lettuce leaves
    rocket
    lamb's lettuce
    spring onions – top and tail and slice thinly
    collection of fresh herbs – cut or chop together
    vinaigrette – recipe on page 86

Wash and spin dry the salad in a salad spinner before breaking into a bowl. Add the prepared onion and herbs and mix together with your hands. Immediately before serving stir in the vinaigrette using 2 wooden spoons to avoid damaging the tender lettuce leaves.

Extra vinaigrette can be served separately.

Tomato and Fresh Basil Salad

    tomatoes
    fresh basil leaves
    sugar
    vinaigrette – recipe on page 86

Layer tomato slices and fresh basil leaves, adding a few pinches of sugar, into a serving dish. Pour vinaigrette over and leave to marinade for 30mins. or longer before serving.

Vinaigrette

Basic recipe
$^2/_3$ sunflower and extra virgin olive oil – mixed
$^1/_3$ vinegar – cider, wine or herb
freshly ground pepper

Put all the ingredients into a jar and shake before serving.

Lazy Cook tips *– make a quantity in readiness for daily use. The flavour and texture can be changed by adding mustards, chopped fresh herbs or chopped onion, balsamic vinegar, concentrated fruit juices etc. Experiment with different flavours to suit your palette.*

Savoury Oatmeal Snack *– makes 6*

75g (3oz) porridge oats
75g (3oz) plain flour
$^1/_2$ teas. baking powder
1 teas. sugar – *optional*
50g (2oz) margarine – softened
2 good tbls. warm water

Topping
cream cheese or pâté
chopped chives or parsley – *optional*
radishes
small salad ingredients
prawns
ham or cold meat

Set oven at gas 4/180°C/160°C fan/Aga baking oven, 3rd runner down.

Follow the method for Oatmeal Biscuits on page 45. Shape the paste into a ball and roll to approx. 5mm ($^1/_4''$) thick and mark into 6 slices. Bake in the pre-set oven for 20–30mins. To serve as a snack spread each biscuit thickly with cream cheese or pâté into which chopped chives have been worked, and top with a selection of the above suggested ingredients or ones of your own choosing.

Savoury Toasts – *makes 4*

> 4 slices toast made from brioche or thickly sliced bread
> sundried tomato paste
> 4 ripe tomatoes – thickly sliced
> freshly ground pepper
> pinch sugar
> fresh basil leaves
> pitted olives – *optional*
>
> *Optional toppings*
> anchovy fillets
> thinly sliced smoked or cooked ham
> cheese slices – cheddar, stilton or parmesan
> whole grain mustard

Set oven at gas 6/200°C/180°C fan/Aga roasting oven, 2nd runner down, or grill.

Spread one side of each bread slice with sundried tomato paste then top with thick tomato slices, sprinkle with sugar and season with freshly ground pepper. Top with the above suggested toppings (or flavours of your own choice), finishing with a cheese slice spread with whole grain mustard and placed mustard side down. Put on an baking tray and bake in a pre-set oven for 10mins. or under a grill – they should be hot throughout before serving.

Lazy Cook tips – *any choice of bread can be used, I do not remove the crusts. If heating under a grill, reduce the temperature after about a minute to ensure all the ingredients will be hot. Ideal as a quick weekend snack.*

Serving Suggestions – *these can be served as a light meal or, made from a smaller bread base, serve as a starter with a little salad. When cooked cut them into small mouth-sized pieces and serve at a drinks party.*

Soups

Guidelines applicable to soup making

Make in advance and when cold store, covered, in a refrigerator or cold larder – use within 4 days. Reheat slowly to boiling point, stirring occasionally. Do not allow the soup to boil once cream has been added – I recommend it is poured into each individual serving or into the tureen.

Purée

some of the modern hand whisks will purée the ingredients in the pan in which they are cooked. This avoids transferring them to a food processor or liquidiser, and extra washing up.

Seasonings

Use pepper and spices and herbs in place of salt.

Serving

In individual hot bowls, a soup tureen or large bowl. Serve with warm bread or rolls.

Soften in water

I often recommend softening onions and other vegetables in a little hot water, this will produce a few concentrated teaspoons of stock which will add goodness and flavour to your recipe without a trace of fat. Soften in a little water only with a lid on the pan. It takes between 1-2mins. depending on the amount of vegetables, being softened.

Celeriac and Sweet Potato Soup – *serves 4*

1 medium sized onion – skin and chop
450g (1lb) approx. celeriac – peel and chop
225g (8oz) sweet potato – peel and chop
600ml (1pt) vegetable or chicken stock
fresh lemon juice
fresh parsley – chopped
single cream – *optional*

Boil a little water in a large pan, add the prepared onion and cook, with lid on pan, until beginning to soften. Add the prepared celeriac and sweet potato and 300ml (10fl.oz) water and simmer for 5–10mins. or until the vegetables have softened. Remove with a slotted spoon and liquidise or process then return to the pan juices. Add 600ml (1pt) vegetable or chicken stock and simmer, with lid on pan, for 10mins. Before serving stir in 1 tbls. fresh lemon juice and a handful of freshly chopped parsley.

Lazy Cook tips – *make in advance of serving (please read **Guidelines** on page 88) and add the parsley before serving. The colour and flavours are excellent. Aga owners should transfer the pan to the simmering oven for the final simmering.*

Celery and Bacon Soup – *serves 4*

1 large onion – skin and chop
$^1/_2$ a head of celery – preferably with green leafy top
1ltr stock
100g (4oz) smoked Black Forest or Parma ham – finely sliced
freshly ground black pepper
a little cream – *optional*

Slice across the celery (approx. 5mm/$^1/_4$" thick), wash and add, with the prepared onion, to a large pan containing a small amount of boiling water. Cook, with lid on pan, for approx. 2mins. or until they begin to soften. Add the stock and simmer, with lid on pan, for 20mins. Season with freshly ground pepper. Remove all fat from the bacon before tearing or cutting into strips and add to the soup. Bring to a simmer, stir in a little cream (optional), and serve.

Lazy Cook tips – *request the ham or bacon is very thinly sliced when purchasing. The final simmering time can be extended to suit your time schedule. If cooking with Aga the simmering should be done in the simmering oven.*

Fridge Tidy Soup

> 1 large onion – skin and chop
> several sticks celery – chop
> 2 teas. piccalilli – cut up chunky pieces
> 1 teas. tomato purée
> mixed dried herbs
> any leftover ends of cooked ham, meat, poultry – cut up
> cooked rice or pasta
> frozen peas
> freshly ground black pepper
> gravy
> stock

Boil a little water in a large pan and add the prepared onion and celery and cook, with lid on pan, until beginning to soften. Add the piccalilli, tomato purée, herbs and pepper and any of the remaining listed ingredients and simmer for 10mins. before serving.

Lazy Cook tips – *if without stock, add a tin of game or vegetable soup*

Parsnip and Mushroom Soup – *serves 4*

> 1 medium onion – skin and chop
> 450g (1lb) parsnips
> 225g (½lb) mushrooms
> 600ml (1pt) vegetable or chicken stock
> freshly ground white pepper
> 1 teas. horseradish cream

Soften the onion in a little boiling water with lid on pan. Top and tail and scrub the parsnips before cutting into chunks. Wipe the mushroom skins with damp kitchen roll before chopping. Add the prepared parsnips, mushrooms and stock to the cooked onion, bring to simmer and simmer for 30mins. with lid on pan. Remove from heat and process or liquidise the vegetables, removing them with a slotted spoon. Pour back into the pan, season with freshly ground pepper, stir in the horseradish cream, bring back to simmer before serving.

Lazy Cook tips – *use dried mushrooms if you do not have fresh ones. Make in advance of serving (please read* **Guidelines** *on page 88). Aga owners should transfer the pan to the simmering oven for the final simmering.*

Parsnip and Watercress Soup – *serves 4*

    1 medium onion – skin and chop
    450g (1lb) parsnips – scrub, top and tail and chop
    600ml (1pt) vegetable or chicken stock
    1 bunch fresh watercress
    2 tbls. single cream – *optional*

Soften the onion in a little boiling water with lid on pan. Add the prepared parsnips and 300ml (10fl.oz) water and simmer for 5–10mins. or until the parsnips have softened. Liquidise or process the parsnips and onion removing them with a slotted spoon, then return to the pan. Add 600ml (1pt) vegetable or chicken stock and simmer, with lid on pan, for 10mins. Chop the watercress, add to the pan and simmer for a couple of minutes. Stir in the cream and serve.

Lazy Cook tips – *make this soup at the beginning of winter when parsnips and watercress are at their best. A good soup with a peppery flavour. Aga owners should transfer the pan to the simmering oven for the final simmering. Make in advance of serving (please read* **Guidelines** *on page 88).*

Spinach and Stilton Flan – *serves 6 slices*

    1 ready baked pastry case – buy
    450g (1lb) spinach – cook (recipe on page 176)
    freshly grated nutmeg
    50g (2oz) Stilton cheese – grated
    150ml (6fl.oz) full cream milk
    2 large eggs

Set oven at gas 4/180°C/160°C fan/Aga baking oven, 3rd runner down.

Put the pastry case on a baking tray and cover the base with the cooked spinach, season with freshly grated nutmeg and scatter with grated cheese. Put the milk into a pan to warm. Whisk the eggs, add the warmed milk and whisk again before pouring through a sieve on to the pastry case ingredients. Cook in the pre-set oven for 20–30mins. or until set and beginning to brown slightly on top. Serve warm or cold with salad.

Lazy Cook tips – *ready-baked pastry cases are available from most delicatessen and supermarkets – a most useful ingredient to keep in store. If fresh spinach is not available buy a bag of frozen and cook as directed on the packet – excellent value and a good ingredient to have in store.*

Terrine – an invaluable ingredient to have in store especially at Christmas and party time.

    225g (8oz) lambs liver
    450g (1lb) pork belly – remove rind
    6 venison (or gamey) sausages – remove skins
    50ml (2fl.oz) red wine
    freshly ground black pepper
    several good pinches mixed dried herbs
    bayleaves – for garnish

Cut the liver and pork into approx. 2cm/1″ cube sized pieces before mixing all the ingredients together – except the bayleaves. Leave to marinade for 2hrs stirring occasionally before packing into one large, or several smaller pots and topping with a bayleaf then a lid. Stand the pot/s in a pan containing enough warm water to come half way up. Put into the pre-set oven (gas 3/160°C/140°C fan/Aga simmering oven) and cook for 1–1½hrs. or until the centre is firm to the touch and the ingredients are shrinking slightly from the sides of the pot/s. Remove and when cold store, covered, in a fridge or cold larder until required. Bring back to room temperature before serving. Eat within 5 days.

Lazy Cook tips – *a terrine is one of those really useful standbys especially at Christmas and other holiday times when unexpected visitors might turn up and suddenly a snack round the kitchen table seems a nice idea. Special pots with lids are available but if you do not have these the terrine can be cooked in a basin or any other ovenproof container and sealed with foil or a tin plate. Although the recipe suggests. marinading for 2hrs, this can be extended to overnight. Stir the ingredients before packing into the pot/s for cooking.*

Main Meals

Poultry and Game   *124*

Guidelines applicable to this section

Coat in seasoned flour

This is done before ingredients are browned or sealed in hot fat. It is important to dry the ingredients first on kitchen roll (wet ingredients will not seal). Coat the ingredients all over in the seasoned flour, then shake off all excess – I do this by tossing the ingredients from hand to hand. Put immediately into the hot fat once they are coated. Ingredients are browned in hot fat to 'seal in' the flavour.

Excess fat

Remove excess fat from hot cooked ingredients by tilting the pan and spooning out the fat/oil. When cooked ingredients are cold all excess fat will rise to the surface, remove it with a knife before reheating.

Heating oil or dripping

Sprinkle a few grains of flour into the pan to test that it is hot enough to take the ingredients to be browned/sealed.

Pots and Pans

I recommend pans that can be used on top of the cooker then put into the oven, this saves a lot of time and washing up. My favourite pans are a large sauté pan with a lid, heavy based saucepans, enamelled cast-iron casseroles and shallow baking dishes, with or without lids. Never add cold liquids to a hot pan.

Reheating from cold

I am a great believer in the saying "yesterday's stew is best". The flavour of many recipes is improved by allowing them to rest for 24hrs. or longer before serving, it gives the ingredients time to blend resulting in an improved flavour. Once cooked the ingredients should be allowed to become cold, covered with a lid or foil, and placed in a refrigerator or cold larder until reheated as follows:

Cover with a lid or foil and put into a hot oven (gas 6/200°C/ 180°C fan/Aga roasting oven) for 10mins. or until it is hot and bubbling – test by spooning out a little from the centre. This is important because often the outer liquid is bubbling but the centre remains luke warm. ***When hot throughout*** reduce the temperature to gas 3/160°C/140°C fan/Aga simmering oven and continue cooking for 10–15mins. or until it is needed for serving. The time will depend on the quantity of ingredients to be reheated. If a single portion is to be reheated this can be done on a hob following the foregoing directions.

Seasonings

Use pepper and spices and herbs in place of salt.

Soften in water

I often recommend softening onions and other vegetables in a little hot water, this will produce a few concentrated teaspoons of stock which will add goodness and flavour to your recipe without a trace of fat. Soften in a little water only with a lid on the pan. It takes between 1–2mins. depending on the amount of vegetables, being softened.

Wine

Boil wine to reduce and to burn off the alcohol leaving the flavour of the wine. This is sometimes done by putting a flame to the hot wine but I do not recommend this method in a domestic kitchen.

When is it cooked?

Poultry – pink chicken and turkey should not be served. Overcooked chicken and turkey is dry and looses much of the flavour. Test by piercing the thickest part with a skewer, it is cooked when the juices run clear.

Meat and Game – with the exception of pork which is cooked when the juices run clear – test by piercing the thickest part with a skewer. Other meats can be cooked to your personal liking, rare, medium or well done. Follow the direction in the recipe and adjust the cooking time accordingly. Game is often casseroled or slow cooked, follow the directions in the recipe or the suppliers instructions.

Offal – liver and kidneys require little cooking – when the blood seeps out they are done. Ox kidney is usually cooked for longer in a casserole or slow cooker.

Meat and Offal

Bangers and Mash with a Pickle Topping
– serves 4

> 12 sausages
> 700g (1¹/₂lb) potatoes – peel and cut into small pieces
> 50g (2oz) butter
> milk
> freshly grated nutmeg
> 1 large jar Pickled red cabbage

Set oven at gas 6/200°C/180°C fan/Aga roasting oven, 2nd runner down.

Place the sausages in a lightly oiled baking tray and bake in the pre-set oven for 15–20mins. or until cooked. Boil the prepared potatoes until they are soft. Strain off the cooking liquid, add the butter, a tablespoon of milk and freshly grated nutmeg and mash until they are creamy and smooth – add more butter or milk if necessary. Pour the cabbage and vinegar into a pan and heat. To serve, pile the potato mash on to individual hot serving plates, top each with three cooked sausages and finally with pickled red cabbage including a little of the vinegar.

Lazy Cook tips *– the sausages can be cooked under a grill. A little milk added to the potatoes will help to cut down on the fat content. Pickled red cabbage adds flavour, colour and a crunchy texture to the traditional Bangers and Mash – it is also quicker than making gravy!*

Beef Slices in a Tomato and Mustard Sauce

– serves 4

A recipe using cheaper cuts

    4 beef slices – not less than 1cm/^{1}/$_2$" thick
    1 tbls. oil or dripping
    1 tbls. flour seasoned with freshly ground black pepper
    4 large shallots (or med. sized onions)
    300ml can of tomato juice
    4 teas. grain mustard
    1 bayleaf
    good sprinkling of mixed dried herbs

Set oven at gas 3/160°C/140°C fan/Aga simmering oven.

Heat the oil or dripping in a sauté or large pan. Remove excess fat before drying meat on kitchen roll. Coat lightly in the seasoned flour then brown on each side in the hot fat. While the meat is browning, skin the onions and leave whole. Remove meat from pan and mop up any excess fat with kitchen roll before adding the tomato juice and mustard and stir, scraping up any residue which may have stuck to the base. Return the meat, onions, bayleaf and herbs, bring to a simmer, cover and put into the pre-set oven for 1^1/$_2$–2hrs. or until the meat is tender. Serve from the pan with vegetables of your choice.

Lazy Cook tips *– a good recipe for using cheaper cuts most of which have an excellent flavour. The fat removed before cooking can be rendered down in a low oven to make dripping (store when cold in a refrigerator). A recipe to make in advance and allow to rest in a refrigerator or cold larder for a day or two before reheating To reheat, cover and put into a hot oven (gas 6/200°C/180°C fan/Aga roasting oven) for 10mins. or until the sauce is simmering. Reduce temperature to gas 3/160°C/140°C fan/Aga simmering oven and continue cooking for 10–15mins. or until it is needed for serving. An ideal recipe if catering for one – re-heat in portions as and when required.*

Braised Beef with Apricots and Black Olives – *serves 4*

A recipe using cheaper cuts

> 4 beef slices – not less than 1cm/¹/₂″ thick
> 1 tbls. olive oil or dripping
> 1 tbls. flour seasoned with freshly ground black pepper
> ¹/₂ bottle red wine
> 100ml (4fl.oz) stock
> 1 teas. sundried tomato paste
> 2 bayleaves
> several sprays fresh thyme (or 1 teas. dried)
> 1 teas. runny honey
> 12–16 whole dried apricots
> 16–20 black pitted olives

Set oven at gas 3/160°C/140°C fan/Aga simmering oven.

Heat the oil or dripping in a sauté or large pan. Remove excess fat before drying the meat on kitchen roll. Coat lightly in the seasoned flour and brown on each side in the hot fat – remove from pan. Add the wine and stock to the pan and scrape up any residue from the base before bringing to boil. Stir in the tomato paste, bayleaves, thyme and honey, return the meat slices, bring to a simmer, cover, and put into the pre-set oven for 1¹/₂–2 hrs. (or until the meat is tender). Towards the end of cooking add the apricots and olives and cook for a further 30mins. To serve, put the meat slices directly on to hot serving plates or down the centre of one large serving dish. Remove the apricots and olives with a slotted spoon and place on top. Boil the remaining sauce until it reduces and begins to thicken, spoon a little over the meat and serve the remainder separately.

Lazy Cook tips – *a good recipe for using cheaper cuts most of which have an excellent flavour. The fat removed before cooking can be rendered down in a low oven to make dripping (store when cold in a refrigerator). A recipe to make in advance and allow to rest in a refrigerator or cold larder for a day or two before reheating.*

To reheat – *please see* **Guidelines** *on reheating on page 96. An ideal recipe if catering for one – re-heat in portions as and when required. Serve within 3 days.*

Serving Suggestions – *I like to serve this with a dish of Roasted Winter Vegetables – potatoes, pumpkin, parsnips and small whole onions (recipe on page 174).*

Braised Silverside Slices with Pickled Walnuts – *serves 4*

4 slices silverside of beef – not less than 1cm/¹/₂″ thick
1 tbls. flour seasoned with freshly ground black pepper
1 tbls. oil
1 medium onion – skin and thinly slice
150ml (5fl.oz) red wine
150ml (5fl.oz)) stock
¹/₂ teas. herbes de Provence
1 teas. grain mustard
8–12 pickled walnuts

Set oven at gas 3/150°C/300°F/Aga simmering oven.

Heat the oil or dripping in a sauté or large pan. Remove excess fat before drying the meat on kitchen roll. Coat lightly in the seasoned flour and brown on each side in the hot fat – remove from pan. Add a little hot water to the pan, scrape up any residue from the base, add the prepared onions and cook, with lid on pan, until they begin to soften, remove from pan and add the wine and stock and boil to reduce by half. Stir in the herbs and mustard and add the meat and onion. Bring to a simmer, cover, and put into the pre-set oven for 1¹/₂–2 hrs (or until the meat is tender). Towards the end of cooking add the pickled walnuts and cook for a further 10mins. To serve, put the meat slices on to hot serving plates or down the centre of one large serving dish. Remove the onion and walnuts with a slotted spoon and place on top and around the meat. Boil the remaining sauce until it reduces and begins to thicken, spoon a little over the meat and serve the remainder separately.

Lazy Cook tips – *a good recipe for using a cheaper cut of meat. The fat removed before cooking can be rendered down in a low oven to make dripping (store when cold in a refrigerator). A recipe to make in advance and allow to rest in a refrigerator or cold larder for a day or two before reheating*

To reheat – *please see* **Guidelines** *on reheating on page 96. An ideal recipe if catering for one – re-heat in portions as and when required. Serve within 3 days.*

Braised Venison – *serves 6–8*
To be prepared 12–24 hours in advance of serving.

> 1¹/₂kg (3¹/₂lb) joint of venison (fillet, haunch, or any cut
>   without bones)
> 2 tbls. plain flour seasoned freshly ground black pepper
> 2 tbls. beef dripping or oil
> 1 tbls. redcurrant jelly
> 12 shallots – skin and leave whole
> 12–16 pitted prunes
>
> *for the marinade*
> ¹/₂ teas. herbes de Provence
> freshly ground black pepper
> 2 good pinches mixed spice
> 2 good pinches ground clove
> 2 dried bayleaves
> 1 lemon – cut into thick slices or quarters
> ¹/₂ bottle red wine

Put the marinade ingredients into a large bowl or basin, add the joint and leave for 12–24hrs. (in a refrigerator or cold larder), turning it every few hours.

To cook – drain the joint from the marinade (see Lazy Cook tips). Heat the dripping or oil in a pan large enough to take all the ingredients. Dry the joint on kitchen roll and coat it in the seasoned flour before adding to the hot fat and browning all over (this may take between 10–15 mins.). Set oven at gas 6/200°C/180°C fan/Aga roasting oven. Remove the joint from the pan and mop up any remaining dripping or oil with kitchen roll. Add hot water to cover the base of the pan and scrape up any residue, add all the marinade ingredients and bring to the boil. Whisk in the redcurrant jelly and reduce to a simmer. Return the joint and the prepared shallots to the pan, bring to a simmer, put lid on pan and place in the pre-set oven for 10–15mins. before reducing the oven temperature to gas 3/160°C/140°C fan/Aga simmering oven, and cook for 1½–2hrs. or until the joint is tender. Towards the end of cooking stir in the prunes.

To serve – remove from oven and put the joint on to a hot serving plate and surround with the solid ingredients (removed with a slotted spoon), discard the bayleaves. Boil the remaining juices for a few minutes until they reduce and begin to thicken. Pour a little over the joint and serve the remainder separately.

Lazy Cook tips – *to drain the marinade juices from the joint before browning, put it into a sieve hanging over the bowl. Do not flour the joint until the fat is hot. The length of cooking time depends on the quality of the joint, a cheaper cut will need longer cooking. A good winter weekend recipe. Can also be made using a joint of beef. Use any remainders as the base for soup.*

Serving Suggestions – *slice to serve. This is a rich meal which I feel needs little more than boiled or jacket potatoes and a green vegetable served with it.*

Cottage and Shepherd's Pies – *serves 3–4*

Traditionally these are made using leftover meat and gravy from a Sunday roast of lamb or beef.

> 450g (1lb) approx. potatoes – peel
> 1 large onion – skin and chop
> 325g (12oz) approx. cooked beef or lamb – minced
> gravy – cooked
> 6 tbls. milk, oil, or melted butter
> freshly grated nutmeg

Set oven gas 6/200°C/180°C fan/Aga roasting oven, 2nd runner down.

Boil the prepared potatoes in a covering of water until they begin to soften, strain off the cooking water. Cover the base of a sauté or large shallow pan with water, bring to boil and add the prepared onion, put lid on pan and cook until the onion begins to soften (1–2mins). Add the minced meat and gravy and stir until simmering before putting into a pie dish. Top with slices of the cooked potato and brush with milk, oil, or melted butter before scattering with freshly grated nutmeg. Put into the pre-set oven for 20–30mins. or until it is hot and bubbling and the potato is browning. Serve straight from the oven with a green vegetable and Worcestershire sauce.

Lazy Cook tips – *the list of ingredients is based on serving 3-4 portions but this depends on the amount of leftover meat and gravy. The cooked meat will be minced in seconds in a food processor. If using lamb, add any leftover mint sauce with the gravy. I slice the cooked potato, I find it quicker than mashing and easier to place on top of the other ingredients. This recipe can be prepared several hours in advance and stored, covered, in a refrigerator or cold larder. Put into the pre-set oven until hot and bubbling before serving. The temperature of the oven can be reduced after 10mins. if you wish to extend the re-heating period. Ring the changes and make with half cooked lamb and half cooked ham. (See also my 'Village Pie' recipe on page 123.)*

Gammon Steaks cooked in a Tomato Sauce

– serves 4

4 gammon steaks
1 tbls. oil
1 large onion – skin and chop
1 x 400g tin chopped tomatoes
good pinch sugar
1 teas. sundried tomato purée or paste
1 tbls. mixed fresh herbs (or 1/2 teas. herbes de Provence)
freshly ground black pepper
fresh basil (or parsley)

Remove and discard all excess fat from the steaks. Heat the oil in a sauté or large pan, add the steaks and cook for a minute or two on each side to brown a little then remove from pan. Add a little water to the pan and scrape up any residue from the base before adding the prepared onion and cook, with lid on pan, until it begins to soften. Stir in all remaining ingredients and bring to a simmer. Return the steaks to the pan and cover with the sauce. Place lid on pan and simmer gently for 10–15mins. Serve direct from the pan or place the steaks down the centre of a hot serving dish, spoon the sauce on top and scatter with cut basil leaves or chopped parsley. Serve with a vegetable of your choice and rice, pasta or couscous.

Lazy Cook tips *– to make a richer sauce add wine or cream (or both) before adding the gammon. Large gammon steaks can be cut into 2 portions, or broken into pieces to make them go further. In the past I have demonstrated this recipe to students illustrating the simplicity and speed of cooking and using the minimum amount of equipment.*

Ham and Leek pie *– serves 6–8*

2 large leeks
freshly grated nutmeg
450g (1lb) cooked ham pieces
1 x 295g tin condensed chicken soup
300ml (10fl.oz) milk
150ml (5fl.oz) stock from the leeks
225g (8oz) wholemeal or shortcrust pastry – bought or
    home-made (recipe on page 65)

Put approx. 300ml (10fl.oz) water to boil in a large pan. Top and tail the leeks, cut into roughly 1cm (1/2″ rings) and wash thoroughly under a cold running water tap before adding to the boiling water and boil for a minute with lid on pan. Strain off and reserve the cooking liquid, put the leeks into a shallow ovenproof dish and grate nutmeg over before topping with the ham pieces. Empty the soup into a pan or basin, add the milk and stock and stir together before pouring over the ham. Roll the pastry to slightly bigger than the dish, place on top and press overhanging pastry into the sides. Use a knife to slash the pastry top several times, stand the dish on a baking tray and put into the pre-set oven for 20–30mins. or until the pastry is beginning to brown slightly. Cover loosely with foil and cook for a further 10mins. before removing from oven and serving. Serve from the dish with vegetables of your choice.

Lazy Cook tips – *use the empty can to measure the milk and stock – one full can measures 300ml (10fl.oz). A good use of leftovers or end pieces of cooked ham – end pieces or thick slices are often available from a delicatessen counter. The liquid remaining from the cooked leeks should give the amount of stock required in the recipe.*

Hot Pot – *serves 4*

700g (1½lb) lamb – cut into chunks
1 tbls. flour seasoned with freshly ground black pepper
300ml (10fl.oz) stock or water
2 medium onions – skin and quarter
1 stalk celery – cut into 1cm/½″ lengths
fresh mint leaves (or or several good pinches dried)
1 teas. mint jelly
700g (1½b) potatoes – peel
1 teas. oil

Set oven at gas 6/200°C/180°C fan/Aga roasting oven, 3rd runner down.

Put the onion and potato into a saucepan, cover with cold water, place lid on pan and bring to boil. Drain off water and keep. Dry the meat on kitchen roll then toss in the seasoned flour. Layer into a casserole or pie dish with half the potatoes (cut into chunks), and the remaining vegetables and herbs and scatter any remaining flour on top. Add the mint jelly and pour in the stock (measured from the reserved vegetable water). Top with the remaining potatoes thickly sliced. Cover with a lid (or foil), and cook for 10–15mins. or until simmering in the pre-set oven then reduce temperature to gas 3/160°C/ 140°C fan/Aga simmering oven and continue cooking for 2–3hrs. or until you are ready to serve it. Remove the lid for the last 30mins. to brown the potatoes. Serve straight from the oven.

Lamb with Garlic Cream Sauce – *serves 4*

4 lamb fillets
a little oil
garlic cream sauce – recipe below

Set oven at gas 6/200°C/180°C fan/Aga roasting oven, 2nd shelf down.

Brush the base of an ovenproof dish with oil, add the fillets and cook in the pre-set oven for 10–15mins. To serve, cut each fillet into slices and arrange on individual hot serving plates. Drizzle with a little of the sauce and serve the remainder separately.

Lazy Cook tips – the length of cooking time will depend on the size of the fillets and whether you prefer them pink or well done. I like to serve this with new potatoes and mangetout – it is one of the quickest meals I prepare but quite delicious.

Garlic Cream Sauce

1 large packet Boursin garlic cream cheese
1 tbls. milk

Put the cheese and milk into a saucepan and whisk over a gentle heat until smooth. Serve hot or cold.

Lambs Kidneys in Peppers – *makes 4*

4 peppers
8 lambs kidneys – cut in half, remove skin and core
8 medium sized flat mushrooms
4 rindless bacon rashers – remove excess fat
2 teas. grain mustard
freshly ground pepper
a little fresh thyme (or a sprinkling of dried)
1 teas. mushroom ketchup
a little butter or double cream – *optional*
oil
cooked rice – *optional* (recipe on page 134)

Set oven at gas 6/200°C/180°C fan/Aga roasting, 3rd second shelf down.

Cut the top from each pepper and carefully remove any inner white flesh and seeds. Cut each half kidney in half, cut each bacon rasher into 4 pieces and thickly slice 4 of the mushrooms and pack all these ingredients into each pepper with the mustard, pepper, thyme and mushroom ketchup, a pat of butter or a teas. of double cream. Top each with a remaining whole mushrooms then with the pepper top. Lightly brush each with oil and stand them in a shallow ovenproof dish. Bake in the pre-set oven for 20–30mins. or until the peppers have softened. Serve straight from the oven on a bed of cooked rice (recipe on pages 134 and 173).

Lazy Cook tips – bake these in a small dish so that they will stand together. The juices which will flow from the pepper once cut into will serve as a sauce to moisten the rice. Any juices from the cooking dish can also be poured over the rice. A colourful meal and full of good flavours.

Main Meals

Minced Beef – to cook

    1 large onion – skin and chop
    450g (1lb) lean minced beef
    1 x 400g tin chopped tomatoes
    pinch sugar
    50ml (2oz) red wine – *optional*
    1 tbls. mixed fresh herbs, chopped (or ½ teas. dried)
    freshly ground black pepper
    few shakings Worcestershire sauce
    garlic – *optional*
    100g (4oz) mushrooms – wipe with kitchen roll and chop

Add water to cover the base of a large pan, bring to boil and add the prepared onion, put lid on pan and cook until the onion begins to soften (approx. 2 mins.), adding a little more hot water if necessary to prevent sticking. Add the minced beef breaking it down with a fork and cook over a gentle heat for 5–10mins. stirring from time to time. Stir in the remaining ingredients and simmer, with lid on pan, for 15–20mins. or until the contents have blended together. Serve hot from the pan, or leave to become cold and store, covered, in a fridge. Use within 4 days removing any fat which will have risen to the top before reheating and serving.

Lazy Cook tips – *this is a most useful ingredient to have in store and will help to make a meal in minutes. I recommend softening the onion in water, or stock to reduce the fat content of the finished dish. Change the flavour by adding some chopped bacon and a teaspoon of mustard. Chopped celery, nuts, olives, or a variety of ingredients of your choice can be added. Minced lamb or pork can also be cooked following this method. If cooking by Aga the final simmering process should be done in the simmering oven.*

Minced Meat Stick – *serves 4–6*

    450g (1lb) cooked minced beef – recipe above
    1 French stick/baguette, or similarly shaped loaf
    several garlic cloves
    1 x 200g packet potato crisps
    50g (2oz) cheese – grated

Set oven at gas 6/200°C/180°C fan/Aga roasting oven, 3rd runner down.

Slice the top from the loaf and tear the bread from the base to form a deep cavity, season with crushed garlic. Fill with hot, cooked mince and top with the crisps crushed by hand into small pieces, and scatter with grated cheese. Put on to a baking tray and bake in the pre-set oven for 10-15mins. Cut into chunks to serve.

Lazy Cook tips – *this recipe is very popular with children and adults alike and will 'stretch' a few ingredients to serve plenty. The mince can be cooked a day or two in advance and stored, covered, in a refrigerator. Remove and discard any fat which will have risen to the top and reheat the mince before adding to the loaf. If packed with hot ingredients it can be finished off under a grill. Make breadcrumbs with the remaining bread, dry them at a low temperature then store in a jar for future use.*

Pork cooked in a Piquant Sauce – *serves 4*

4 spare rib steaks
1 tbls. flour
1 tbls. freshly chopped sage leaves (or 1 teas. dried)
freshly ground black pepper
1 tbls. oil
1 medium sized onion – skin and chop
1 teas. sundried tomato purée, or paste
1 tbls. Worcestershire sauce
1 tbls. cider vinegar
1 teas. Dijon mustard
1 tbls. fresh lemon juice
1 tbls. demerara sugar
300ml (1/2pt) stock or red wine (or a mixture of both)

Set oven at gas 3/160°C/140°C fan/Aga simmering oven.

Trim all excess fat from the steaks before drying on kitchen roll. Heat the oil in a sauté pan. Mix the sage and freshly ground pepper into the flour and lightly coat each steak. Add to the hot oil and cook for about a minute on each side or until beginning to brown then remove from pan. Add a film of hot water to the pan and scrape up all residue from the base before adding the prepared onion and cook, with lid on pan, until it begins to soften (about a minute). Stir in the remaining ingredients, add the steaks and bring to a simmer. Cover and cook in the pre-set oven for 30–40mins. or until the steaks are tender (test with a metal skewer). Serve on to hot plates or put down the centre of a hot serving dish. Boil the sauce to reduce a little before pouring over the steaks. Serve with a vegetable of your choice and rice.

Lazy Cook tips – *this recipe can be cooked on the top of the cooker, cover and keep at a gentle simmer (occasional bubble) until the steaks are tender.*

Pork Steaks with an Orange and Ginger Sauce – *serves 4*

4 spare rib steaks
1 tbls. flour seasoned with freshly ground white pepper
1 tbls. oil
1 small onion – skin and finely chop
150ml ($1/4$pt) white wine
150ml ($1/4$pt) concentrated orange juice
1 teas. grated (or shavings) root ginger
1 tbls. double cream

Set oven at gas 3/160°C/140°C fan/Aga simmering oven.

Heat the oil in a sauté or large pan. Dry the steaks on kitchen roll, remove all fat and lightly coat in the seasoned flour. Add to the hot oil and brown for about a minute on each side then remove from pan. Add a little hot water to the pan, scrape up any residue from the base, add the prepared onion and cook, with lid on pan, until it begins to soften (about one minute), remove from pan. Add the wine and orange juice and boil, without lid, until it reduces a little. Stir in the ginger, return the steaks and onion and any remaining juices, bring to a simmer, cover and cook in the pre-set oven for 30–40mins. or until the steaks are tender – test with a metal skewer. Remove from the oven and put the steaks on to individual hot plates or on one hot serving dish. Stir the cream into the sauce and bring to a simmer. Pour a little over the steaks and serve the remainder separately. Serve with vegetables of your choice.

Lazy Cook tips – *I use spare rib steaks for this recipe although it is equally good made with slices of pork fillet. Can be prepared in advance and stored when cold, covered, in a fridge or cold larder. Serve within 3 days. Reheat to simmering before serving (see* **Guidelines** *on page 96).*

Roast Lamb with an Aubergine Filling and Mint Gravy – *serves 6*

$^1/_2$ shoulder of lamb – boned
1 aubergine
several sprigs of fresh rosemary
600ml (1pt) stock (or a mixture of stock and red wine)
1 tbls. mint jelly

Set oven at gas 6/200°C/400°F/Aga roasting oven, high runner.

Lay the joint skin side down and remove any visible excess fat. Top with thin slices of aubergine. Roll up tightly and secure with metal skewers or tie with string. Weigh the joint and assess the roasting time by allowing 20mins. per 450g (1lb) and 20mins. resting time after roasting. Put a trivet into a roasting tin and cover with rosemary sprigs. Place the prepared joint on top and add water to cover the base of the tin. Put into the pre-set oven and reduce the temperature after 30mins. to gas 4/180°C/350°F/Aga baking oven, for the remainder of the roasting time. Remove from oven and lightly cover with foil and allow the joint to rest for 15–20mins. before transferring to a hot serving dish. Remove the trivet from the tin, add the stock or wine (or both), scrape up any residue from the base and boil for a few minutes to reduce. Whisk in the mint jelly and bring back to boiling point before pouring into a hot gravy or sauce boat to serve.

Lazy Cook tips – *allow an extra 20mins. roasting at the lower temperature for a more well done meat. Slice to serve, with a vegetable of your choice and roast potatoes. The gravy can be thickened with plain flour made into a smooth paste with cold water and added to the tin to boil.*

Main Meals

Roast Lamb with Kidneys – *serves 8*

1 lamb joint
1 lamb's kidney per person
fresh rosemary sprigs
600ml (1pt) stock (or a mixture of stock and red wine)

Set oven gas 6/200°C/400°F/Aga roasting oven, high runner.

Weigh the joint and assess the roasting time by allowing 20mins. per 450g (1lb) and 20mins. resting time after roasting. Put a trivet into a roasting tin and scatter with fresh rosemary before placing the joint on top and adding water to cover the base of the tin. Put into the pre-set oven and reduce the temperature after 30mins. to gas 4/180°C/350°F/Aga baking oven, for the remainder of the roasting time. Prepare the kidneys as described on page 138 and 5 mins. before the joint is to be taken from the oven remove any excess fat from the tin and put the kidneys (cut side down) into the remaining juices, around and beneath the trivet. Return tin to oven and continue roasting for 5mins. Remove from oven and lightly cover with foil and allow the joint to rest for 10–15mins. before transferring to a hot serving dish placing the kidney halves around or to one end. Remove the trivet, add the stock or wine (or both) to the tin, scrape up any residue from the base and boil for a few minutes to reduce. Pour into a hot gravy or sauce boat to serve.

Lazy Cook tips *– a shoulder or leg joint is ideal for this recipe. In addition to these flavours blending well together this is an excellent way of stretching a joint to serve extra portions. Allow an extra 20mins. roasting at the lower temperature for a more well done meat. The gravy can be thickened with plain flour made into a smooth paste with cold water before adding to the tin to boil.*

Savoury Meat Batter – *serves 6*

> 300ml (10fl.oz) batter mixture – recipe below
> 1 tbls. oil
> 1 medium onion – skin and chop
> 450g (1lb) minced beef

Set oven at gas 6/200°C/400°F/Aga roasting oven, 2nd runner down.

Make the batter mixture and leave to rest as directed in the recipe. Heat 1 tbls. oil in a large, shallow, ovenproof dish in the pre-set oven. Add the prepared onion and mince, breaking it down with a fork, return to oven and cook for 5–10mins. Whisk 1 tbls. cold water into the batter mixture and pour it over the mince. Return to the oven and cook for 20–30mins. or until the batter has risen at the edges and is browning. Serve straight from the oven, cut into wedges, with tomato ketchup or HP sauce, and frozen peas.

Lazy Cook tips – *a popular family meal which will stretch a small quantity of mince to feed many.*

Batter/Yorkshire Pudding mixture

> 100g (4oz) plain flour
> 300ml (½pt) milk
> 2 large eggs
> 1 tbls. oil

Put the flour, milk, eggs and oil into a food processor or liquidiser and process for a few seconds until smooth. Cover and put into a refrigerator or cold larder for a minimum of 30mins. to thicken. Before cooking whisk in a little cold water from a running tap. Follow individual recipes for oven temperatures and cooking times.

Lazy Cook tips – *the recommended resting time allows the starch grains in the flour to swell and thicken the batter. The addition of cold water will give off a steam during cooking which will lighten the batter. When serving as Yorkshire pudding with roast beef, I pour the batter into the roasting tin*

Simmering of Meats – to feed a crowd

An invaluable recipe for weekend entertaining when there seems a constant need for meals and little time in which to prepare them, and relax, and enjoy the weekend activities. The method of cooking ensures a succulent, juicy texture to the ingredients.

1¹/₂kg (3¹/₂lb) ham or bacon piece
2kg (4¹/₂lb) chicken
900g (2lb) sausages
bunch of mixed fresh herbs (or a bouquet garni of dried herbs)
2 bayleaves
12 black peppercorns
12 whole cloves

Put all the ingredients into a pan and cover with cold water. Bring *slowly* to a gentle simmer with the lid partly covering the pan – this should take at least one hour. Place lid fully on pan and continue gently simmering for 30mins. Test that the cooking is complete by piercing the thickest part of the chicken leg with a skewer, the juices will run clear when it is cooked.

Lazy Cook tips *– clearly a very large pan is required to hold all the ingredients. A preserving pan can be used, using foil as a lid. It is most important that the initial simmering process is done slowly in order for the heat to penetrate all the ingredients and the time will vary depending on the weight of the ingredients. If cooking by Aga once the initial simmering point is reached, continue the remaining simmering process in the simmering oven. Use all the stock for soups and sauces.*

Serving Suggestions

To serve hot – *carve the ham and the chicken and arrange on a large hot serving dish with the sausages sliced diagonally. Spoon some of the stock from the pan into a smaller pan, bring to a boil and whisk in a tablespoon of tomato purée, a pinch sugar and some mixed chopped herbs and serve this separately as a sauce.*

To serve cold – *once the initial gentle simmering is achieved, remove the pan from the heat, cover completely with the lid and leave until cold then store in a refrigerator or cold larder until needed. Serve the carved cold slices scattered with cress, and serve with salad and new potatoes and mayonnaise.*

Lazy Cook tips – *any remaining ingredients can be disguised following other recipes in this book. Alternatively Chicken with Apricots and Almonds, or Spicy Chicken (recipes in 'Lazy Cook in the Kitchen' ISBN 0954231910). Turkey and Mushroom Bake (recipe in 'A Lazy Cook's Christmas' ISBN 0954231929).*

"I'm not cooking!"

"I'm not cooking" was first said to us by a waitress after we had rejected the tired looking sandwiches on display in the plastic cabinet at the seaside "caff" typical of British holiday resorts in the '70's.

We were cold, wet and hungry; the children were noisy and looked about to start a fight, if you know what I mean! I asked if we might have something hot, beans on toast would do, to which came the aforementioned reply. Beans on toast, she considered to be cooking. I couldn't believe it!

Little did I realise that many years later I might share the sentiments of that obviously overworked and overtired waitress. But I do, and often, and at such times I cook one of the laziest meals I know – steak, oven chips and frozen peas – with sauce! Do try it (recipe on page 117).

Sirloin Steaks with a Peppered Cream Sauce – *serves 4*

4 Sirloin steaks no less than 1cm/½" thick
oil
freshly ground black pepper
peppered cream sauce – recipe below

Heat a sauté or large frying pan. Dry the steaks on kitchen roll then brush one side with oil and season with freshly ground black pepper before adding to the hot pan. Time the cooking according to whether you like it rare, medium or well done (please refer to my recommendations below). Before turning the steaks, oil and season the second side. Remove from pan and put on to individual hot plates or one large serving dish, and spoon any remaining juices over each steak. Serve the sauce separately.

Lazy Cook tips – *recommended cooking times:*
2mins. on each side to cook rare
3mins. "   "   "   "   medium rare
5mins. "   "   "   "   well done

Peppered Cream Sauce

1 large packet Boursin peppered cream cheese
1 tbls. milk

Put the cheese and milk into a saucepan and whisk over a gentle heat until smooth. Serve hot or cold.

Steak Kidney and Mushroom Pie – to prepare a

day in advance of serving – *serves 6–8*

Prepare the following ingredients (except the pastry), a day before the pie is to be served:

> 700g (1½lb) stewing steak – cut into mouthsized pieces
> 225g (8oz) ox kidney – trim off fat, cut kidney into small pieces
> 2 tbls. plain flour seasoned with freshly ground black pepper
> ½ teas. Marmite
> 2 dried bay leaves
> 450g (1lb) mushrooms
> 1 teas. mushroom ketchup
> 1 tbls. plain flour for thickening – *optional*
> 225g (8oz) shortcrust or wholemeal pastry (bought or
>   home-made, recipe on page 65)

Set oven at gas 6/200°C/180°C fan/Aga roasting oven.

Lightly coat the steak and kidney in seasoned flour before putting into an ovenproof casserole with the bay leaves. Stir the marmite into 300ml (½pt) boiling water, pour into the casserole and stir, cover and place in the pre-set oven for 10–15mins. or until it begins to simmer. Reduce the oven temperature to gas 3/160°C/140°C fan/Aga simmering oven, and cook until the meat is tender (this is best done slowly and could take up to 2 hours or longer). Towards the end of cooking slice and stir in the mushrooms and mushroom ketchup. Blend 1 tbls. plain flour to a smooth paste with cold water and stir this into the casserole. Cover and continue cooking for 20–30mins. Remove from oven and make into a pie following the instructions below. Alternatively, remove lid from the cooked ingredients and allow to become cold. Cover and store in a refrigerator or cold larder in readiness for making into a pie.

To make into a pie

Set oven at gas 6/200°C/180°C fan/Aga roasting oven, 2nd runner down.

Remove and discard any fat which may have risen to the surface of the casserole. Place a pie funnel (or egg cup) in the centre of a pie dish

118

and using a slotted spoon, put the casserole ingredients in and around with some of the gravy. Roll the pastry to 5mm/¼″ thickness. Oil the rim of the pie dish and cover with strips of pastry, press down and moisten with water. Cover with the remaining pastry pressing down on the rim. Trim away any surplus pastry then, using a blunt knife, seal the layers together by knocking against the edges. Press a damp fork all round the top rim, cut a cross in the centre, place in a baking tin and bake in the pre-set oven for 30–40mins. or until the pastry has cooked and the ingredients are hot and bubbling.

Lazy Cook tips – *once the pastry has cooked you may need to reduce the oven temperature and bake for a little longer until the pie ingredients are hot (this is especially so if covering cold ingredients). If you wish to decorate the pastry top before baking, cut 4 leaves from the leftover pastry pieces and arrange these around the cross in the centre, moisten them with water to make them stick in place. Heat the remaining gravy and serve this separately. Always popular and an excellent meal to pack to serve on the first night of a self-catering holiday. Take the cooked ingredients in a sealed polythene bag and make into a pie as directed.*

Steaks with an Artichoke and Apricot Compote – *serves 4*

    4 beef steaks – sirloin, rump or fillet
    1 tbls. oil
    25g (1oz) butter
    2 tbls. brandy
    1 jar sliced artichokes in oil
    8 ready to eat dried apricots
    fresh thyme

Trim any excess fat from the steaks before drying them on kitchen roll. Heat a large frying or sauté pan. Brush the steaks with oil and add to the pan and cook for 2–5mins. on each side, add the butter and when sizzling add the prepared steaks. Cook for 2–5mins. on each side. Meanwhile prepare the compote by draining the artichokes from the oil and chopping them roughly with the apricots. Remove the cooked steaks from the pan and keep warm. Add the brandy, scrape up any residue from the base of the pan before bringing to a boil. Add the prepared compote, reduce the heat and stir the compote until hot, season with thyme leaves. Put the steaks on hot individual plates, add any remaining juices to the compote and stir in then serve alongside the steaks.

Lazy Cook tips — *the amount of cooking time depends on the thickness of the steaks and whether you prefer them rare, medium or well done. Ripe, fresh apricots can be used in summer, also whole artichokes bought by weight from a delicatessen. If fresh thyme is not available use dried.*

Serving Suggestions — *Serve with new potatoes and a mixed green salad for a delicious summer meal. Serve with oven chips or jacket potatoes and a green vegetable in winter.*

Stew and Dumplings – *serves 6*

700g (1½lb) thick slices of shin or leg of beef
50g (2oz) plain flour seasoned with freshly ground black pepper
2 tbls. oil (or 50g/2oz beef dripping)
450g (1lb) onions – skin and slice into rings
1 bayleaf
1 ltr (1¾pts) hot water or stock
dumplings (recipe below)

Set oven at gas 3/160°C/140°C fan/Aga simmering oven.

Heat half the oil or dripping in a large saucepan. Dry the meat on kitchen roll before lightly coating in seasoned flour, add it to the hot fat and brown on each side then remove from pan. Scrape up any residue from the base of the pan, add the remaining oil or dripping and when hot add the prepared onion rings. Stir well then scatter with the remaining seasoned flour, place lid on pan and cook for 2mins. stirring occasionally. Return the meat to the pan with the bayleaf and hot water or stock. Stir and bring to boiling point then reduce to a gentle simmer (occasional bubbles), put lid on pan and continue simmering in the pre-set oven for 1½-2hrs. or until the meat is tender. Thirty minutes before serving drop the dumplings into the simmering stew. Replace the lid and continue to cook for thirty minutes **without raising the lid**.

Lazy Cook tips – *this recipe can be completely cooked on a gentle simmering hob (occasional bubbles). Thick slices of shin of beef (or leg of beef as it is now often sold) is, I believe, the only meat with which to make stew and dumplings. The flavour is excellent and the strings of gristle running through the flesh adds a rich glutinous texture. Cut the slices into smaller pieces if preferred but using large slices speeds up the browning process. Dumplings should be light in texture. My late mother-in-law taught me the secret is not to lift the lid once they have been added and to allow 30mins for them to cook to perfection. I recommend the stew is made a day or two before it is to be served and stored when cold in a fridge or cold larder. Remove any fat which has risen to the top before reheating. Bring slowly to boiling point, (stirring occasionally) then reduce to a gentle simmer before adding the dumplings (see main recipe).*

Serving Suggestions – *straight from the pan or put on to a heated serving dish, scatter with freshly chopped parsley and surround with boiled potatoes and carrots.*

Dumplings – *makes 8–12*

100g (4oz) plain flour
1 heaped teas. baking powder
freshly ground white pepper
50g (2oz) shredded suet
cold water to mix

Mix all the dry ingredients together in a basin using a blunt knife then mix to a sticky paste under a cold running tap. Turn on to a lightly floured board, cut into 8 or 12 pieces and shape each into a ball in the palm of your hand, lightly floured. Add to a gently simmering stew and cook for 30mins. **without lifting lid**.

Toad in the Hole – *serves 6*

600ml (1pt) batter mixture – recipe on page 114
12 pork sausages
25g (1oz) pork dripping or 1tbls. oil

Make the batter and leave in refrigerator for 30mins. as instructed in the recipe. Set oven at gas 6/200°C/180°C fan/Aga roasting oven, 2nd runner down.

Put the dripping (or oil), into a large shallow ovenproof dish (or roasting tin), and heat in the hot oven. Add the sausages and cook for 10mins. Whisk two tablespoons cold water into the made batter then pour this into the baking dish with the sausages. Continue to cook for 15–20mins. or until the batter has risen and is crisp round the edges. Remove from oven and cut into wedges and serve directly from the baking dish on to hot serving plates.

Lazy Cook tips – *I prefer the batter cooked crisp at the edges and slightly soft in the centre. Serve with Tomato Ketchup or HP sauce for a good family meal. If making for children choose chipolata or cocktail sausages and cook in patti tins as follows – heat a little oil in each hole, add one sausage to each (cut in half if using chipolatas), and cook in the hot oven for 5–10mins. before pouring in the made batter. Cook for 5–10mins. or until the batter has risen. Remove from tin and allow to cool a little before serving to children. These are also good served at a drinks party – serve individually in a serviette. See Fish in Batter recipe on page 26.*

Village Pie – *serves 6*

1 large onion – skin and chop
450g (1lb) minced beef
225g (8oz) chicken livers
1 x 400g tin chopped tomatoes
pinch of sugar
2fl.oz red or white wine, or stock
freshly ground black pepper
mixed herbs – fresh or dried

Topping
750g pkt. frozen oven chips

Set oven at gas 6/200°C/180°C fan/Aga roasting oven, high runner.

Cover the base of a sauté or large shallow pan with water and bring to boil. Add the chopped onion, put lid on pan and cook for 1–2mins. or until the onion softens. adding a little more hot water if necessary to prevent sticking. Add the minced beef breaking it down with a fork and cook over a gentle heat for 5–10mins. stirring from time to time. Stir in the remaining ingredients (except the oven chips), and simmer, with lid on pan, for 5–10mins. or until the contents have blended together. Put into a large shallow ovenproof dish and top with oven chips. Put into the pre-set oven for 20–30mins. or until the chips have browned a little and the ingredients are hot and bubbling. Serve with frozen peas and fresh carrots, or vegetables of your choice.

Lazy Cook tips – *a really quick meal to prepare and one which will be popular with all the family – a good recipe to serve to a crowd – quickly! Prepare the ingredients in advance and store, covered, in a refrigerator or cold larder, top with the chips and cook as directed in the recipe. Please read* **Guidelines** *on page 96.*

Poultry and Game

Chicken and Bacon Rolls with Sundried Tomatoes – *serves 4*

4 chicken breasts
12 rashers lean rindless streaky bacon
1 jar sundried tomatoes in oil
few pinches dried tarragon
150ml (5fl.oz) stock or wine
2 teas. sundried tomato purée

Set oven at gas 6/200°C/180°C fan/Aga roasting oven, 2nd runner down.

Prepare each roll as follows – stretch 3 bacon rashers with a knife and place slightly overlapping. Top with 3 sundried tomatoes, a sprinkling of dried tarragon and a chicken breast then roll up. Lightly brush the base of an ovenproof pan with oil, add the chicken rolls placing the loose bacon ends down and cook in the pre-set oven for 10–15mins. or until when pierced through the centre with a metal skewer the juices run clear. Place on a serving dish or individual plates. Add stock or wine, and tomato purée to the pan juices, stir together and boil until reduced and becoming syrupy, pour over each chicken roll and serve.

Lazy Cook tips *– please read the **Guidelines** applicable to cooking chicken on page 97. Serve hot or cold with vegetables or salad.*

Chicken Fingers

Cut chicken breasts into strips and arrange them over the base of a lightly oiled shallow ovenproof dish. Scatter with fresh or dried breadcrumbs and top with a scattering of oil. Bake in a hot oven (gas 6/200°C/400°F/Aga roasting oven, 2nd shelf down) for 10–15mins. or until the chicken is firm or when pierced with a skewer the juices run clear – please read **Guidelines** on page 97. Cool a little before serving as individual fingers.

Lazy Cook tips *– a good recipe to serve to children. Also serve as a starter or light meal.*

Chicken Legs with Lime *– serves 4*

> 1 tbls. oil
> 4 chicken legs
> 4 small onions – skin and cut into quarters
> 1 lime – zest and juice
> 150ml (5fl.oz) stock or white wine

Set oven gas 4/180°C/160°C fan/Aga baking oven, 3rd runner down.

Heat the oil in a sauté or shallow ovenproof pan. Add the legs and brown, skin side down. Remove from pan and add the onions, toss in the oil, put lid on pan and cook for 1–2mins. then remove from pan. Drain and discard all oil from the pan and wipe with kitchen roll before pouring in a smear of hot water and scrape up all residue from the base. Add the stock and wine and boil to reduce by half. Add half the zest and 2tbls. lime juice, the legs and onions and bring to a simmer. Put lid on pan and put in the pre-set oven for 30–45mins. or until the legs are tender, test with a skewer. To serve, put the legs on individual hot plates or one large serving dish and put the onion on top and around (remove from the pan with a slotted spoon). Boil the remaining juices until they reduce and begin to thicken. Stir in the remaining zest and spoon a little over the legs and serve the remainder separately.

Lazy Cook tips – *if the sauce is too sharp, stir in a ¹/₂ teas. runny honey. Can be made in advance and reheated – please read the **Guidelines** applicable to cooking chicken and reheating, on pages 96 and 97. Remove the zest from lime before squeezing out the juice. A colourful meal and full of good flavours and textures This recipe can be cooked on the top of the cooker at a 'gentle' simmer.*

Chicken Splits – to serve 4

    4 chicken breasts
    2 tbls. oil
    1 tbls. flour seasoned with freshly ground white pepper
    4 large flat mushrooms – wipe with damp kitchen roll
    150ml (5fl.oz.) chicken or vegetable stock
    1 teas. mushroom ketchup

Heat the oil in a large sauté or frying pan. Dry the breasts on kitchen roll then lightly coat in the seasoned flour. Brown in the hot oil for approx. 5mins on each side, remove pan from heat and loosely cover with foil to keep the breasts warm. While the breasts are browning poach the whole mushrooms by adding them to the stock with a teaspoon of mushroom ketchup, bring to a simmer and simmer, with lid on pan, for 2–3mins. or until the mushrooms soften. To serve, cut two splits in each breast, cutting from the thick side, cut each mushroom in half and place in the splits, cut side inside. Add the mushroom juices to the pan in which the chicken was cooked, scrape up any residue from the base then boil to reduce a little before pouring over each chicken split.

Lazy Cook tips – *please read the* **Guidelines** *applicable to cooking chicken on page 97. Handle the hot cooked mushrooms with kitchen tongs. These are also good filled with cooked pepper slices, or a combination of both.*

Chicken Thighs with Banana and Bacon
– serves 4

> 4 chicken thighs with skin
> 4 thin slices Parma or Black Forest bacon – remove fat
> fresh or dried thyme
> 2 small bananas – peel and cut in half
> 1 tbls. oil
> 1 tbls. flour seasoned with freshly ground white pepper
> 150ml (5fl.oz) chicken stock
> 50ml (2oz) brandy
> 1 tbls. single cream – *optional*

Set oven at gas 3/160°C/140°C fan/Aga simmering oven.

Using a sharp knife remove the bones from the thighs and any excess fat, but not the skin. Put the thighs, skin side down, and scatter with thyme. Roll each piece of banana in a slice of bacon and put on the thighs, close and secure with a wooden cocktail stick, overlapping the skin if possible. Heat the oil in a sauté or shallow ovenproof pan. Lightly coat each prepared thigh in seasoned flour and brown all over in the hot fat then remove from pan. Add the stock and brandy to the pan and scrape up any residue which may have stuck to the base. Boil until reduced by half. Return the thighs to the pan, add the ginger, cover and cook in the pre-set oven for 30–40mins. the juices will run clear when the chicken is cooked – pierce with a skewer to test. Place on individual or one large hot serving dish and cover with foil to keep warm. Remove any excess fat from the pan, add the cream, bring to a simmer and serve separately.

Lazy Cook tips – *please read the **Guidelines** applicable to cooking chicken on page 97. When making these if it is difficult to pierce through the skin with the cocktail stick, snip it with scissors. Stem ginger preserved in syrup can be used. Remove excess fat from the pan juices by tilting the pan and spooning it out. Stock can be made by simmering the chicken bones and fat from the bacon in a little water for 30mins. to one hour – strain into a basin and when cold store in a refrigerator. Use within 4 days or freeze.*

Last Minute Chicken Casserole – *serves 6–8*

> 1 pkt. of 10 chicken thighs (with bone)
> 8 thick rashers rindless bacon – remove excess fat and cut each
>   rasher into 3 pieces
> 400g tin chopped tomatoes
> pinch sugar
> 1/2 teas. dried herbes de Provence
> 1/2 teas. dried tarragon
> freshly ground black pepper
> 2 cloves garlic – skin and chop
> 100g dried sundried tomatoes
> 300ml (10fl oz) stock (or a mixture of stock and red wine)

Set oven gas 6/200°C/180°C fan/Aga roasting oven, low runner.

Remove excess skin from the thighs. Put all the ingredients in the order in which they are listed into a casserole arranging the sundried tomatoes on top. Cover and put into pre-set oven for 20–30mins. or until simmering – test by spooning a little liquid from the centre. Reduce temperature to gas 3/160°C/140°C fan/Aga simmering oven and continue to cook for 15–20mins. or until the chicken is cooked and tender (test with a skewer). Remove and discard all excess fat by tilting the pan and spooning it out. Serve from the casserole, with mixed mash or rice, or pasta, and a green vegetable of your choice.

Serving Suggestions – *an ideal recipe if cooking for one. Reduce the ingredients recommended and re-heat in portions as and when required. Use within 4 days.*

Light and Dark Chicken with Fresh Peaches – *serves 4*

340g pkt. mini chicken breast fillets
400g pkt. chicken livers
oil
1 tbls. flour seasoned with freshly ground white pepper
25g (1oz) butter – *optional*
4 tbls. brandy
2 peaches
fresh thyme
2 tbls. double cream – *optional*

Heat a tbls. oil in a sauté or large frying pan. Dry the chicken on kitchen roll before lightly coating in the seasoned flour. Add to the hot oil and cook for 1–2mins. on each side – remove from pan and loosely cover with foil to keep warm. Scrape up any residue from the base of the pan, add the butter (or 1 tbls. oil). Cut and discard any fatty bits from the livers and dry them on kitchen roll before adding to the pan and cook for 1–2mins. on each side, remove from pan and loosely cover with foil to keep warm. Add the brandy to the pan scraping up any residue from the base and bring to the boil. Cut the peaches in half and remove the stones then cut each half into 3 slices and simmer in the brandy for 2–3mins. adding the thyme during cooking. Serve on individual hot plates, placing the livers alongside the chicken pieces and top with peach slices. Add any juices drained from the chicken and livers to the pan, stir in the cream and bring to a simmer before pouring over the peaches.

Lazy Cook tips – *please read the **Guidelines** applicable to cooking chicken on page 97. Turn the chicken livers as soon as blood seeps from them, overcooking spoils the delicate flavour. A colourful recipe packed with goodness and individual flavours.*

Serving Suggestions – *serve on individual hot plates or pile on to one large hot serving plate and allow your guests to help themselves. I like to serve this recipe in the summer with new minted potatoes and mangetout.*

Puffed Up Chicken with a Tapenade Sauce

– serves 4

> 4 skinless chicken breasts
> 1 sheet ready rolled puff pastry
> Tapanade (olive paste)

Set oven at gas 7/220°C/200°C fan//Aga roasting oven, 2nd runner down.

Lightly oil a baking tray or tin. Cut the sheet of pastry into 4 and spread a teas. tapanade down the centre of each. Top with a chicken breast and enclose it in the pastry (like a sausage roll). Put on to the prepared tray, loose pastry ends down, prick across the top with a fork then bake in the pre-set oven for 10–15mins. or until the pastry has risen and browned slightly. Serve immediately with a Tapanade Sauce – recipe on page 131.

Lazy Cook tips – *it adds to the presentation if the chicken breasts slightly protrude from the pastry at each end. So quick to prepare and cook – a good* recipe to serve when entertaining, Children will enjoy these when the tapenade might be replaced with tomato purée or paste, and they are served with tomato sauce – straight from the bottle or following my recipe on page 27. The pastry helps to keep the breasts moist, test that they are cooked by piercing the centre of the pastry towards the base. Please read **Guidelines** on page 97. I recommend frozen ready-rolled puff pastry – an invaluable ingredient to have in store in a freezer.

Tapenade Sauce

50ml (2fl.oz) white wine
50ml (2fl.oz) vegetable or chicken stock
2 teas. tapenade paste
fresh fennel fern – if available
2 teas. double cream

Put the wine and stock into a pan and boil to reduce by half. Stir in the remaining ingredients and serve.

Lazy Cook tips – *if making this sauce to serve with fish use fish stock. Shred the fennel from one spray of fern to make tiny strands. Can be stored, when cold, in a refrigerator or cold larder, covered. Use within 3 days. Tapenade paste is available from supermarkets or delicatessen.*

Roast Chicken for One

1 whole chicken weighing not less than 1^1/$_2$kg (3lb)
butter or oil
parsley and thyme forcemeat – recipe on page 25
sausagemeat – remove the skin from 2–3 sausages

Set oven at gas 6/200°C/180°C fan/Aga roasting oven.

Cut through the skin of the chicken following the line of the breast bone. Loosen the skin and peel back then remove each breast Fill the cavities with parsley and thyme stuffing and sausagemeat (or fillings of your choice). Bring the skin back to cover the fillings and secure with a metal skewer or by sewing with strong thread or fine string. Weigh the chicken and assess the roasting time allowing 20mins. per 450g/1lb and 15mins. resting time after cooking. Spread butter over the skin, including the legs (or brush with oil), and place the chicken on a trivet in a roasting tin. Pour approx. 300ml (10fl.oz) hot water into the tin. Roast in the pre-set oven for 15mins. then reduce the temperature to gas 4/180°C/160°C fan/Aga baking oven for the remainder of the assessed roasting time – test by piercing the thickest part of the leg with a cocktail stick or skewer and if the juices run clear the chicken is cooked (please refer to **Guidelines** on page 97). Remove from oven, cover loosely with foil and leave for 15mins. before carving.

Lazy Cook tips – *this recipe enables those catering for one, or couples, to enjoy a roast without feeling they will be eating cold chicken for days afterwards. Removing of the breasts is easily done and these can be frozen individually or together for use in another recipe. Mushroom and Tomato Forcemeat (recipe on page 136) can be used as an alternative filling.*

Serving Suggestions – *hot, with roast potatoes and parsnips, a green vegetable, and gravy (recipe below). English mustard and cranberry sauce. Serve cold with salad or make into sandwiches.*

Gravy – to serve with a roast

Blend 1–2tbls. plain flour to a smooth paste with cold water. Add to the juices in the roasting tin (once the joint and trivet have been removed). Add a few spots gravy browning and stir over a hot heat until boiling. Thin to required consistency with vegetable stock and simmer until needed for serving.

Lazy Cook tips – *if the juices in the pan are too fatty, tilt the pan and spoon out all excess fat before adding the gravy ingredients. The amount of flour will depend on the thickness of the gravy preferred. Can be flavoured with wine, add with the thickening. Any leftover gravy should be stored, covered, in a refrigerator or cold larder. It can be used for adding to Fridge Tidy soups (recipe on page 90).*

Turkey – roast

Set oven at gas 6/200°C/180°C fan/Aga roasting oven.

Add a chosen stuffing to the turkey before placing it on a trivet in a large roasting tin. Smear butter or oil over the skin and pour approx. 600ml (1pt) boiling water into the pan. Put into the pre-set oven and roast for 30mins. Remove from the oven and cover completely with foil. Return to oven and reduce the temperature to gas 4/180°C/160°C fan/Aga baking oven for the remainder of the assessed roasting time (see notes on 'roasting time' below). Remove from oven, remove the foil (taking care, hot steam may escape), and test by sticking a metal skewer into the thickest part of the leg, if the juices run clear the turkey is cooked. if not, return it to the oven and continue roasting and testing every 10mins. (please read **Guidelines** on page 97). Remove from oven when cooked, loosen the foil and allow the turkey to rest for 20–30mins. before putting on to a hot serving dish and carving.

Lazy Cook tips – the juices from the pan should be kept. Pour them into a basin and when cold store them in a fridge or cold larder. They provide excellent stock for soups, sauces, bakes or casseroles. Remove any fat which will have set on the surface, before using. Use within 4 days or freeze.

Roasting Time

Add the approximate weight of a chosen stuffing to the weight of the turkey (without giblets). Assess the roasting time allowing 15mins. to each 450gm (1lb) and add 20–30mins. resting time before the turkey is carved. For example, a turkey (including stuffing) weighing 6kg (13½lb) should need approximately 3hrs. 20mins. roasting time. After roasting allow the turkey to rest for 30mins. before it is carved. As with all roasts, this allows the juices which have risen during roasting to fall and keep the meat moist.

Turkey Curry – *serves 6–8*

450g (1lb) cooked turkey meat
curry sauce – recipe on page 135
450g (1lb) rice – cook – recipe below

Break the turkey into mouthsized pieces and add to the curry sauce. Bring to a simmer and continue simmering, with lid on pan for 5–10mins. or until hot throughout.

Lazy Cook tips – *it hardly seems Christmas without the 'pickings' from the turkey carcase served in a curry sauce. The one I suggest is rich but very good – an excellent last minute party recipe.*

Serving Suggestions – *pile on top of a rice base on individual hot plates or one large serving dish. Serve with the accompaniments of your choice.*

Rice – to cook

Put the rice into a sieve and shake under a cold running tap until thoroughly washed. Half fill a large saucepan with water, bring to boil and shake in the washed rice. Stir until gently simmering (occasional bubble), put lid on pan and gently simmer for 15-20mins. or until cooked. Pour into the sieve and rinse under a cold water tap to serve cold, or pour a kettle of boiling water over if the rice is to be served hot.

Lazy Cook tips – *the cooked grains should remain whole, tender and separate. Store, covered, in a refrigerator or cold larder. Use within 3 days. I cook with short grain brown rice. A most nutritious and useful ingredient to have in store for last-minute meals. See also recipe on page 173.*

Curry Sauce

50g (2oz) butter
1 medium onion – skin and chop
50g (2oz) plain flour
2 teas. tomato purée
1–2teas. curry powder – hot or medium
600ml (1pt) stock
300ml (½pt) single cream

Heat half the butter in a large saucepan, add the onion, put lid on pan and cook for 1–2mins. or until the onion is softening. Add the remaining butter and when melted stir in the flour, tomato purée and curry powder and cook over a gentle heat, stirring occasionally, for approx. 2mins. Pour in the stock and stir over a gentle heat until it simmers and simmer until it begins to thicken – add more stock if it is too thick. Before serving stir in the cream and the chosen ingredient and simmer for 5–10mins. or until it is hot throughout.

Pâté – Pastes

Mushroom and Tomato Forcemeat

175g (6oz) bread
2 large flat mushrooms
freshly ground black pepper
6 sundried tomatoes – from a jar preserved in oil
1 large egg
3–4 good pinches dried tarragon

Set oven at gas 4/180°C/160°C fan/Aga baking oven, 3rd runner down.

Break the bread into a processor and process into crumbs. Add the remaining ingredients and process to a sticky paste. Spread into a lightly oiled ovenproof baking dish and bake in the pre-set oven for 10–15mins.

Lazy Cook tips *– if more liquid is needed add a few spots mushroom ketchup or a little water. If time allows let the ingredients rest for 30mins. before baking. Can be used as a stuffing for poultry and game. Can be shaped into balls and served individually.*

Preparation of Ingredients

Guidelines appropriate to this section

Use a sharp knife and work on a chopping board or similar surface.
Slice a small piece from a spherical shaped ingredient to form a flat
surface. Put the ingredient on the board, flat surface down, to avoid
any movement when cutting into smaller pieces or slicing.

Cabbage (green and red) – remove any outer damaged leaves. Stand the cabbage on the root end and cut into quarters. Cut away the solid root from each quarter and discard. Turn each quarter on to a cut side and slice through the leaves, thickly or thinly, as required.

Carrots – scrub the skin. Top and tail and if long, cut the carrots into 2 or 3 lengths.

To shape into *strips/juliennes*, stand the whole carrot, or cut length, on its end. Cut into half then cut each half into three or four strips.

To dice, stand the carrot or cut length on its end. Cut down to the base but not through each length, first into quarters, then into eights, depending on the size of the dice required. Turn the carrot on to its side and cut down finely or thickly as needed. Cut the end pieces to the size of the remainder.

Eggs
To separate – working over a basin or similar container, crack the shell into two halves. Toss the contents between the halves allowing the white to drop into the basin.

To shell when hard-boiled – crack the shell. Using the handle end of a spoon, push this between the shell and the egg and peel the shell away.

Grapefruit – cut the fruit in half. Using a grapefruit knife, cut down each segment to separate it from the membrane.

Kidneys (lambs or pigs) – slice the kidneys in half from the core end. Peel off the outer skin. Grip the core between finger and thumb and cut it out using a sharp knife or scissors.

Mango – the flesh is very slippery and I find the following is the best way to prepare them. Peel and discard the skin from one half. Slice the flesh until the course flesh around the stone is reached, scrape this with a knife to remove all excess juice. Do the same with the remaining half.

Preparation of Ingredients

Mushrooms – wipe the skin with damp kitchen roll. Leave whole, slice or quarter as the recipe requires.

Onions – cut the top off the onion and peel the skin away down to the root end – ***do not cut this off*** because it is from here that the milky juices escape and cause sore eyes.

To chop – stand the onion on the root end and cut down this far **but not through the root**, into quarters, eigths, sixteenths, depending on how roughly or finely chopped the onion is needed. Turn the onion on its side and cut down as finely or thickly as is needed. With a little practice you will find this method of preparing onions quick, easy and tearfree!

Peppers – cut around the top (the stalk end). Squeeze the pepper and the top then the top and inside seeds can be lifted out in one piece.

Pineapple – cut off the top and the end. Stand the pineapple on one end and cut off and discard the spikey skin. Remove and discard any bits which remain in the pineapple using the point of a potato peeler.

To cut into rings – turn the skinned pineapple on its side and slice to the desired thickness. Remove the centre stalk from each ring using a small pastry cutter.

To cut into chunks – pile the pineapple slices together and cut through to the required size.

Swede – this is a very solid vegetable and requires care in preparation. Peel and discard all outer skin. Cut a slice from the whole swede and put it cut side down on to a chopping board. Using a knife with a long blade, press on the handle and the tip of the blade to make the initial cuts. Cut the swede in half and putting each half cut side down, slice thickly and then cut each slice into chunks.

Puddings

Additional pudding recipes included in Main Index on page 184

Baked Christmas Pudding (using leftovers)

cold Christmas pudding
brandy
brandy sauce – recipe below

Set oven gas 3/160°C/140°C fan/Aga simmering oven, 3rd runner down.

Put slices of the pudding in a shallow ovenproof dish, scatter with brandy then spread with brandy sauce. Bake uncovered in the pre-set oven until hot throughout.

Lazy Cook tips – baking time depends on how quickly you need the pudding, it can be left in the oven for an hour or more or, at a higher temperature it will be ready for serving in 10–15mins. A good way of using up leftover pudding and sauce, very delicious, very 'Lazy Cook'.

Brandy Sauce

600ml (1pt) full cream milk
2 desst. cornflour
1 desst. sugar
brandy – a liberal amount

Mix a little of the milk and cornflour to a smooth paste. Put the remaining milk into a pan and heat. Add the cornflour paste and brandy and stir until it boils. Remove from heat, add sugar to taste and serve with Christmas pudding.

Lazy Cook tips – this can be made in advance and reheated for serving. Store when cold, covered, in a refrigerator or cold larder.

Baked Summer Fruits Topped with Pink Meringue – *serves 6*

wash a selection of the following fruits before preparing:
2 peaches – cut in half, remove and discard the stone
2 nectarines – cut in half, remove and discard the stone
225g (8oz) strawberries – remove and discard stalk
225g (8oz) raspberries – remove and discard stalk
4 apricots – cut in half, remove and discard stone
1 tbls. dark muscavado sugar
2 teas. orange flower water
4 tbls. brandy
2 egg whites
100g (4oz) caster sugar
few spots pink food colouring – *optional*

Set oven at gas 4/180°C/160°C fan/Aga baking oven, 3rd runner down.

Put the prepared fruit into a pie dish and scatter with the sugar then sprinkle with orange flower water and brandy. Make the meringue topping by whisking the whites and food colouring at a high speed until they are stiff and dry, (a cottonwool texture). Reduce the speed whilst slowly pouring in the sugar until it has all whisked in. Spread to completely cover the fruit and touch the sides of the dish. Stand the dish on a baking tray and bake in the pre-set oven for 5–10mins. or until the meringue begins to brown then reduce the oven temperature to gas 3/160°C/140°C fan/Aga simmering oven and continue baking for 20–30mins. or until it is needed for serving.

Lazy Cook tips – *a lovely pudding to make when the the summer fruits are at their best. Please refer to notes on meringue making on page 152.*

Banana and Ginger Trifle

700ml (25fl.oz) full cream milk
2 rounded desst. custard powder
1/2 desst. sugar
few spots vanilla extract
1 pkt. trifle sponges – split each into 2
3 large bananas
2–3 pieces stem ginger
284ml (10fl.oz) double cream
ready grated chocolate

Mix the custard powder to a smooth paste with a little of the milk, heat the remainder in a pan with the vanilla extract and sugar. Add the paste and stir until boiling. Remove from heat and allow to cool a little. Make the trifle by layering the sponges, banana slices, ginger pieces and custard into a dish, ending with custard. Leave to become cold before spreading with whipped cream and scattering with grated chocolate.

Lazy Cook tips – *the made custard should be of a runny consistency so that it soaks into the sponges. If serving this to children you might choose to omit the ginger. A delicious trifle and so easy to make. Store when cold, covered, in a refrigerator or cold larder and bring back to room temperature before serving.*

Crumbly Apple Flan – *serves 6–8*

1 ready baked pastry case
450g (1lb) Bramley cooking apples
75g (3oz) jumbo oats
4 tbls. golden syrup
grated zest of 1 lemon
good squeeze lemon juice

Set oven at gas 4/180°C/160°C fan/Aga baking oven, 3rd runner down.

Put the pastry case on a baking tray. Peel, core and slice the apples into the flan case. Put the golden syrup, lemon juice and zest into a pan over a gentle heat and when melted stir in the jumbo oats. Spread on top of the apple slices and bake for 20–30mins. in the pre-set oven. Serve hot, warm or cold with ice cream, cream or custard.

Lazy Cook tips – *the flan is cooked when the apples are soft, test with a skewer.*

Fresh Fruit Meringues

> meringues
> double cream – whipped
> fresh fruit of your choice

Make a meringue mixture following the recipe on page 152 and drop from a tablespoon on to the prepared baking tray and bake or dry as directed. To serve, sandwich together with whipped cream and the chosen fruit, whole or sliced. Pile on to a serving dish.

Lazy Cook tips – *whole strawberries or raspberries; apricot, nectarine or peach slices are all delicious served in meringues. The meringue shapes can be made in advance and stored in a polythene bag – they should remain crisp for a week. If serving at an outdoor informal party, wrap them in individual serviettes.*

Fresh Fruit Salad for early summer – *serves 6*

> 1 Galia (or similar) melon
> 4 ripe nectarines – wash
> 225g (8oz) ruby seedless grapes – wash
> 10–12 fresh mint leaves
> 2 teas. rose water

Cut the melon in half and remove the centre seeds. Using a teaspoon, spoon out the flesh into a large basin catching all the juices as they flow from the melon. Cut the nectarines in half and remove and discard the stones, slice the flesh directly into the bowl of melon, add the grapes. Cut the mint leaves into strips and scatter over the fruit. Add 2 teas. rose water and mix all together by hand or using two wooden spoons to avoid damaging the fruit.

Allow to rest for 30mins or more before serving.

Lazy Cook tips – *a deliciously refreshing salad to serve before the main crop of summer fruits is available.*

Fresh Fruit Salad for winter with a Honey and Vanilla Syrup – *serves 4*

50ml (2oz) warm water
1 teas. runny honey
$1/4$ teas. vanilla extract
1 medium mango – peel and slice (see page 138)
2 ripe pears – peel, core and slice
225g (8oz) ruby seedless grapes – wash

Make the syrup by dissolving the honey and vanilla essence in warm water. Prepare the fruit directly into a serving bowl, or individual dishes and pour the syrup over. Allow the fruit to marinade in the syrup for 20–30 mins. before serving.

Lazy Cook tips – *this syrup can also be used for other fruit salads.*

Fresh Pineapple Rings with a Honey and Brandy Syrup – *serve 4–6*

1 large pineapple
1 teas. runny honey
1 tbls. brandy
$1/2$ teas. rose water

Make the syrup by putting a little hot water into a measuring jug and stirring in the honey, brandy and rosewater until dissolved. Top up to 75ml (3oz) with cold water. Prepare the pineapple rings as described on page 139. Arrange the rings in a serving dish, pour on the syrup and leave for an hour or more before serving.

Lazy Cook tips – *use a sharp knife to prepare the pineapple.*

Fresh Strawberry Sponge – *serves 8*

For the sponges
3 large eggs
75g (3oz) caster sugar
75g (3oz) plain flour
a little extra caster sugar

For the filling
284ml (10oz) carton of double cream
2 tbls. milk
225g (8oz) fresh strawberries
icing sugar

To make the sponges

Set oven at gas 3/160°C/140°C fan/Aga simmering, oven low runner.

Put the eggs and sugar into a mixer bowl, with the whisk or beaters (not plastic), and put into the oven to warm (this should take 3–4mins. only). Meanwhile oil or line with bake-o-glide one large or 2 small baking trays, weigh and sieve the flour. Remove the bowl from the oven and increase the oven temperature to gas 6/200°C/180°C fan/Aga baking oven. Using an electric hand mixer, whisk the warmed ingredients at top speed until they are of a thick consistency (like spreading cream). Sieve the flour again then stir it into the egg mixture. Spread on to the prepared tray/s into rounds approx. 25cm/10″ in diameter and scatter the tops with caster sugar. Bake in the pre-set oven for 6–10mins. or until turning a biscuit colour. Remove from oven and transfer immediately to a wire cooling tray (use a large palette knife to remove). If not for immediate use store them when cold in an airtight container or large polythene bag. Use within 1 week or freeze.

To assemble into a Fresh Strawberry Sponge

Whip the cream and milk together until a soft, spreadable consistency and sandwich the sponges together with this and the strawberries cut into thick slices – reserving one strawberry to put on the top. When assembled sieve with icing sugar.

Lazy Cook tips – *this makes a most delicious pudding and because it uses a fatless sponge mixture it is not too rich. With practice the sponges are easily made and are a most useful confection to have in store. I doubt you are able to buy anything resembling them. I find it best to spread the whipped cream on to each sponge plate, add the strawberries to one and then top with the second – sugar side up. Experiment using other fillings.*

Sponge Drops – *makes approx. 24*

Make up a 2 egg quantity following the directions in the main recipe on page 146. Drop the mixture from a dessertspoon on to the prepared baking tray/s, scatter each with caster sugar and bake in the pre-set oven for 4–5mins. or until they turn a pale biscuit colour. Cool and store as directed in the main recipe.

Serving Suggestions – *as a biscuit or sandwiched together with cream and jam or fresh strawberries as a pudding.*

Fruit Alaska – *8–10 slices*

> 1 large ready baked sponge flan case – buy
> 1 x 750ml carton vanilla ice cream
> 450g (1lb) frozen fruits and berries
> 4 egg whites
> few spots pink food colouring – *optional*
> 225g (8oz) caster sugar

Set oven at gas 6/200°C/180°C fan/Aga roasting oven, 3rd runner down.

Place the flan case on a baking tray lined with bake-o-glide or lightly oiled. Fill the centre cavity with the ice cream and top with the frozen fruits. Whisk the egg whites and food colouring at high speed until they are stiff and dry (of a cottonwool texture). Reduce the speed whilst slowly pouring in the sugar until it has all mixed in. Spread to completely cover the filling and touch the sides of the flan and bake immediately in the pre-set oven for 5–10mins. or until the meringue begins to brown. Turn the oven off and after 5mins. remove the flan from the oven and ease from the baking tray on to a serving dish using a long palette knife or fish slice and serve immediately.

Lazy Cook tips – *when the pudding is served the fruits should be firm though de-frosted, test with a metal skewer and if necessary return to a warm oven for 5–10mins. If you cook by Aga, once the meringue top has browned transfer to the simmering oven for 5–10mins. before serving. With all the ingredients in store, this pudding is quickly assembled between courses. A great family favourite. Please refer to notes on meringue making on page 152.*

Fruit Brulée – *serves 4–6*

> 450g (1lb) fresh soft fruits including seedless grapes
> 1/4 teas. vanilla extract – optional
> 284ml (10oz) carton double cream
> 225g (8oz) soft brown sugar

Wash the fruit before putting it into a shallow ovenproof dish and add the vanilla. Whisk the cream to a spreading consistency and spread over the fruit then put it into a refrigerator to chill for an hour or more. To serve, cover with sugar and place under a hot grill until the sugar has caramelised.

Lazy Cook tips – *this can be made using just one fruit or a mixture, all must be seedless. If you do not have a grill, caramelise the sugar using a kitchen blow torch.*

Fruit and Custard

600ml (1pt) full cream milk
1 desst. granulated sugar
$^{1}/_{4}$ teas. vanilla extract
4 large eggs – whisked together
25g (1oz) butter – *optional*
freshly grated nutmeg – *optional*
184ml (10fl.oz) double cream
225g (8oz) fresh strawberries, raspberries or summer fruits

Set oven at gas 4/180°C/160°C fan/Aga baking oven, 3rd runner down.

Warm the milk, sugar and vanilla in a pan before pouring it on to the whisked eggs then pour it, through a sieve, into a 850ml (1½pt) souffle dish, or 6 ramekin dishes. Top with a little butter and freshly grated nutmeg. Stand the dish/es in a roasting tin and add warm water to come approximately half way up. Bake in the pre-set oven for 10mins. before reducing the temperature to gas 3/160°C/140°C fan/Aga simmering oven, until the custard has set. Remove from the oven, lift out of the tin and leave until cold. To serve, cover with whipped cream and top with whole strawberries, raspberries or any soft summer fruits and serve.

Lazy Cook tips – *the custard can be baked in advance and stored, covered, in a fridge or cold larder – eat within 4 days. To make the quantity of cream go further, add 2tbls. milk during whipping. This is an example of my even lazier recipes, what was Upsidedown Trifle in 'A Lazy Cook's Summer' is now reduced to plain though equally delicious "Fruit and Custard".*

Fruit Custard Tart – *serves 6–8 slices*

1 ready baked pastry case
100g (4oz) pitted prunes
150ml (5fl.oz) full cream milk
1 teas. sugar
1 teas. cornflour
2 large eggs
grated nutmeg

Set oven at gas 4/180°C/160°C fan/Aga baking oven, 3rd runner down.

Stand the flan on a baking tray and arrange the prunes over the base. Mix the cornflour to a smooth paste with a little cold milk and put into a pan with the remaining milk and sugar and stir over a gentle heat until it has warmed. Whisk the eggs, add the milk mixture and whisk again before pouring it, through a sieve, on to the prunes. Scatter with freshly grated nutmeg and bake in the pre-set oven for 20-30mins. or until set. Cool on a wire tray. Serve warm or cold with or without single cream or vanilla ice cream. A small glass of ginger wine is nice served with this pudding.

Lazy Cook tips *– this flan can be made using most dried fruits. Add a little more sugar to the custard if you wish, or sweeten with honey. Leave the flan in the foil case while cooking the filling. Store, covered, in a fridge or cold larder. Eat within 4 days. Ready baked pastry cases are available from most delicatessen or supermarkets in shortcrust or wholemeal pastry.*

Fruit in Batter – see recipe on page 26

Lazy Lemon Meringue Pie – *serves 6–8*

1 ready baked pastry case
1 x 411g jar lemon curd
2 lemons – juice and zest
75g (3oz) dried breadcrumbs (recipe below)
2 egg whites
100g (4oz) caster sugar
little yellow food colouring – *optional*

Set oven at gas 4/180°C/160°C fan/Aga baking oven, 3rd runner down.

Put the pastry case on a baking tray. Empty the lemon curd into a bowl and add the juice and zest of both lemons, and the breadcrumbs, and stir together before spreading into the pastry case. Make the meringue by whisking the egg whites and food colouring at high speed until they are stiff and dry (a cottonwool texture). Reduce the speed whilst slowly pouring in the sugar until it has all mixed in. Spread this to cover the lemon filling and touch the edge of the pastry case. Bake in the preset oven for 5–10mins. (or until the meringue begins to brown), then reduce the temperature to gas 3/160°C/140°C fan/Aga simmering oven and continue to bake for 30mins. or until you wish to serve the pie. Serve hot or warm with single cream or ice cream.

Lazy Cook tips – *I recommend at least 4 tablespoons lemon juice is added to the lemon curd, if the lemons are not very juicy more than 2 may be needed. Remove the zest from the lemons before squeezing. Dried breadcrumbs will give a lightness to the texture of the filling. Please refer to notes on meringue making on page 152. Ready cooked pastry cases are available from supermarkets and delicatessen – I find them an invaluable store-cupboard ingredient for sweet or savoury fillings.*

Dried Breadcrumbs

Crumb bread in a food processor or liquidiser. Place on a tin tray and dry until crisp in a cool oven or on top of an Aga. Store in jars. An invaluable ingredient to have in store.

Meringues

Experience has taught me that successful meringue making comes not from the age or the temperature of the eggs but from the whisking of the whites before sugar is added – this should be stiff and dry and the texture of cotton wool – dense and pure white. Meringues of varying shapes and sizes are an invaluable ingredient to have in store. I store them in polythene bags and find they will remain crisp for several months.

To make a basic meringue mixture

To each egg white allow 50g (2oz) caster sugar. Whip the whites until they are stiff and dry (I describe this as a cottonwool texture), before whisking in the sugar. The meringue is then ready to be shaped, or piped, on to baking trays covered with household parchment or bake-o-glide. When shaped, put into a low oven to dry (gas 2/ 150°C/130°C fan/Aga simmering oven possibly with the door slightly ajar) or follow the temperature quoted in a recipe. They are dry when they will peel from the lining paper. Allow a few minutes for the meringue shapes to become cold before storing in airtight containers, or polythene bags.

Meringue toppings – when meringue is used as toppings for pies, e.g. lemon meringue pie, they are usually placed in a hot oven – gas 6/ 200°C/180°C fan/Aga roasting oven for 5-10mins or until they begin to brown Some recipes recommend the oven temperature is then reduced for longer cooking – the longer the meringue is cooked at a low temperature the more crisp it will become.

Lazy Cook tips – if a bubbling of liquid appears in the cooked meringue this is because the sugar has not been completely mixed into the whisked whites. This will add a slightly toffee texture to the meringue. Cream, which is the most popular ingredient to serve with meringues, will soften the texture and make for ease of slicing.

Meringue Shapes

Bases and Plates

Spread the meringue into rounds or rectangular shapes in the sizes required. A four egg white meringue mixture will shape 2 x 25cm/10″ in diameter round bases.

Rings

Spread the meringue into rings of the size required leaving a centre cavity. A three egg white meringue mixture will shape 2 x 25cm/10″ rings.

Petites Meringues

Drop the meringue from a tea, dessert or tablespoon (depending on the size required) or shape through a piping bag.

Oatcake Slice with Raspberry Cream

– serves 6–8

> 100g (4oz) margarine
> 75g (3oz) self-raising flour
> 100g (4oz) porridge oats
> 50g (2oz) demerara sugar
> 284ml (10fl.oz) double cream
> 225g (8oz) fresh raspberries

Set oven gas 4/180°C/160°C fan/Aga baking oven, 3rd runner down.

Lightly oil an 18cm (7″) sandwich tin. Melt the margarine in a large pan over a gentle heat. Remove from heat and stir in the flour, oats and sugar. Press into the prepared tin and bake in the pre-set oven for 25–30mins. or until beginning to brown. Remove from oven and cut into 6–8 slices before allowing to cool.

When cold arrange the slices on to a round gateau or serving platter and spread with the cream lightly whipped then top with the raspberries.

Lazy Cook tips – *top with any summer fruits or berries. Make the base in advance and store in an airtight container, use within one month.*

Plum and Almond Pudding – *serves 6–8*

50g (2oz) self-raising flour
50g (2oz) caster sugar
25g (1oz) ground almonds
50g (2oz) margarine – softened
1 large egg
1/4 teas. almond extract
450g (1lb) plums – wash, cut in half and remove stones
1 desst. demerara sugar for topping

Set oven at gas 4/180°C/160°C fan/Aga baking oven, 3rd runner down.

Oil a shallow cake tin (approx. 18cm/7″ in diameter). Put the flour, sugar and ground almonds into a food processor and process for a few seconds. Add the margarine, egg and almond essence and process until smooth. Spread into the prepared tin and cover with the plum halves (cut side down). Scatter with demerara sugar and bake in the pre-set oven for 30–45mins. or until firm to the touch. Serve hot or warm with cream, ice-cream or custard. When cold serve as a cake.

Lazy Cook tips – *stand the tin on a baking tray to bake in case the ingredients spill over. Choose Victoria plums if available. The texture is slightly soggy, the flavours are good. All the cake ingredients can be mixed in a large bowl with a wooden spoon or electric whisk.*

Plums in Pimm's – a grown-up jelly! – *serves 6*

450g (1lb) Victoria plums – wash, cut in half, remove stones
350ml (12 fl.oz) water
1 sachet gellatine (a skimp $^1/_2$oz)
200ml (8fl.oz) Pimm's No. 1
1 tbls. runny honey

Put the prepared plums into a glass serving dish. Put 50ml (2fl. oz) hot water into a measuring jug, sprinkle in the gellatine and stir or whisk until dissolved. Make up to 350ml (12fl.oz) with hot water and stir in the honey and when dissolved stir in the Pimm's. Pour over the plums and when cold cover and put into a fridge or cold larder to set.

Lazy Cook tips – *leaf gellatine can also be used for this recipe – follow the manufacturer's directions for dissolving.*

Raspberry Choux Buns – *makes 10*

Choux pastry shapes – recipe below
184g (10fl.oz) double cream
450g (1lb) fresh raspberries
icing sugar

Shape and cook the choux buns as directed in recipe below. Fill with whipped cream and raspberries and sieve with icing sugar.

Lazy Cook tips – *the choice of filling can be varied, they are good filled with most summer fruits.*

Choux Pastry

150ml (5fl.oz) cold water
50g (2oz) butter
75g (3oz) plain flour
2 large eggs

Set oven at gas 6/200°C/180°C fan/Aga roasting oven, 2nd runner down.

Put the water and butter into a pan and heat slowly until the butter has melted, increase the heat and when the liquid rises in the pan add the flour and beat until the mixture leaves the side of the pan. Remove from heat and leave to cool a little before adding the eggs and beating until the mixture is smooth. Lightly oil a baking tray and put tablespoons of the pastry on, spaced well apart. Bake in the pre-set oven for 15–20mins. or until they have puffed up and are crisp. Remove from oven and using a pointed knife, make a slit in each to allow steam to escape and remove and discard all uncooked paste. Serve immediately or freeze when cold.

Lazy Cook tips – *take great care when slitting the cooked choux, hot steam escapes. Choux pastry is mostly associated with éclairs or profiterole, but it has many other uses, savoury and sweet. It is a quick and easy pastry to make. The mixture can be made and kept in a refrigerator for several hours before it is baked. Always bake it in a hot oven and serve as soon as possible after it has baked, it should be crisp and light in texture. Cooked choux shapes can be frozen – as they begin to thaw pop them into a hot oven for a few minutes to bring back to a crisp texture.*

Raspberry Ripple Melba – *makes 4*

several scoops of raspberry ripple ice-cream
225g (8oz) fresh raspberries – wash
raspberry fruit syrup or raspberry liqueur – *optional*
284ml (10oz) carton double cream
ginger thin biscuits
grated chocolate

Put scoops of ice-cream into individual stemmed glasses and top with some of the raspberries then sprinkle with raspberry syrup or liqueur.

Lightly whip the cream and fold in the remainder of the raspberries and 8-10 crushed ginger thin biscuits and pile this into each glass. Top with a Ginger Thin biscuit and scatter with grated chocolate. Serve immediately.

Lazy Cook tips – *have all the ingredients ready to assemble. I recommend Charbonnel et Walker Chocolate Charbonnel for instant grated chocolate. A refreshing summer pudding and stretches a few raspberries to serve many.*

Rhubarb Jelly with Raspberry Cream – *serves 6*

1 pkt. raspberry flavoured jelly cubes
2 serving spoons of cooked rhubarb and juice
(5fl.oz) double cream
225g (8oz) fresh raspberries

Break the jelly cubes into a measuring jug. Make up to 300ml ($^1\!/_2$pt) with boiling water and stir until the cubes have dissolved. Stir in the cooked rhubarb and 2 extra serving spoons of rhubarb juice. Make up to 650ml (1pt, 2fl.oz) with more boiling water. Pour into a mould or dish and leave to set. To serve, spread the jelly with whipped cream and top with raspberries.

Lazy Cook tips – *a jelly packed with good fruit flavours and ideal for summer serving. Can be made using gelatine crystals or leaf gelatine – follow the manufacturer's instructions to make up.*

Rhubarb Perfumed with Rosemary and Lavender

700g (1$^1\!/_2$lb) rhubarb
1 teas. orange flower water
1 tbls. lavender honey
1 sprig rosemary

Set oven at gas 4/180°C/160°C fan/Aga baking oven, 3rd runner down.

Top and tail the rhubarb, wash, and cut into approximately 2cm/1″ lengths. Put into an ovenproof dish with 1 tbls. cold water, the orange flower water and honey and top with the rosemary sprig. Cover and cook in the pre-set oven for 20–30mins. or until soft. Serve with Vanilla and Ginger ice cream.

Lazy Cook tips – *I use rhubarb in sweet and savoury recipes. It's well worth finding a place amongst the flower beds to grow a little of your own. Best pulled in the early summer and forgotten after the end of July.*

Sauces and Syrups

Savoury Sauces

Sweet Sauces

Syrups

Vegetables

Guidelines appropriate to this section

Boil in the minimum amount of water and keep this after cooking to use as vegetable stock. Store it when cold, in a refrigerator or cold larder. Use within 3 days.

Preparation – when cutting vegetables put a flat side down so that the vegetable sits firmly as you cut through it. Use a sharp knife and a chopping board.

Roast in the minimum amount of oil or fat made hot before the vegetables are added.

Saucepan – choose a large saucepan, with a fitting lid even for boiling small quantities.

Wash all vegetables thoroughly before cooking – with one exception – mushrooms which I recommend are carefully wiped with damp kitchen roll.

When are they cooked?

Very much a matter of choice as to whether you enjoy them cooked al dente or soft – test with a metal skewer.

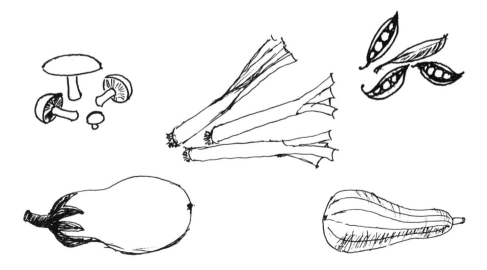

Antipasto of Roasted Vegetables and Rosemary – *serves 6–8*

I enjoy serving this best in summer when the rosemary is shooting new growth and after picking the fragrance remains on my fingers.

> 1 large aubergine
> 3 large peppers (red, yellow and green)
> several sprigs of fresh rosemary
> 450g (1lb) small dark mushrooms
> 1 teas. mushroom ketchup
> 1 jar artichoke hearts (or pieces) in oil
> 1 jar sundried tomatoes in oil

Set oven at gas 6/200°C/180°C fan/Aga roasting oven, high runner.

Heat the oil in a roasting tin in the pre-set oven. Prepare the peppers by removing and discarding the stalk and inside seeds then cut each pepper into quarters. Put into the hot oil, skin side up. and lightly oil the skin side only. Top and tail the aubergine and slice lengthways into 5-6 slices. Put into the tin with the peppers and lightly brush all over with the remaining oil, scatter rosemary sprigs over the top. Bake in the pre-set oven for 20–30mins. or until they begin to brown, remove from oven and put into a serving bowl. While the vegetables are roasting cook the mushrooms – wipe the whole mushrooms with damp kitchen roll and put them into a pan containing very little water and 1 teas. mushroom ketchup. Simmer, with lid on pan, until they have softened, add to the vegetables and boil any remaining juices until reduced to about a tablespoon and add to the vegetables. Leave all until cold before stirring in the artichokes and sundried tomatoes both drained from the oil. Scatter with the cooked rosemary sprigs. Serve immediately or store, covered, in a refrigerator and use within 4 days.

Lazy Cook tips *– this method of preparation uses the minimum of oil. These flavours will give a delicious and colourful start to a summer meal or picnic. Encourage everyone to 'mop up' with bread between courses then only one plate per person is needed throughout the meal. If cooking by Aga the mushrooms should be brought to a simmer on the simmering hob then transferred to the simmering oven. This recipe will reheat well from cold, put* *into an ovenproof dish (including juices) and heat for 10–15mins. at gas 6/200°C/180°C fan/Aga roasting oven 2nd shelf down. This is especially useful if when cooking a hot meal oven space is limited.*

Baked Aubergine – *serves 2*

1 large aubergine
a little oil
1 medium onion – skin and chop
100g (4oz) mushrooms – chop
1 teas. mushroom ketchup
1 teas. sundried tomato paste
freshly ground white pepper
4–6 sundried tomatoes – cut into strips
several good pinches mixed dried herbs (or 1 teas. mixed fresh)
2 tbls. breadcrumbs – fresh or dried
50g (2oz) grated cheese

Set oven at gas 6/200°C/180°C fan/Aga roasting oven, 3rd runner down.

Wash and top and tail the aubergine then cut in half lengthways. Remove the flesh and keep. Score the flesh side of the aubergine and brush this and the skin with oil before placing skin side down, in a shallow ovenproof dish. Bake in the pre-set oven for 20–30mins. or until the skin has softened. Meanwhile prepare the filling by adding the chopped onion to a pan containing a little boiling water or stock, place lid on pan and cook until the onion begins to soften. Cut the aubergine flesh into small cubes and add to the onion with the prepared mushrooms, mushroom ketchup, and sundried tomato paste. Season with freshly ground pepper, stir, and cook for 2–3mins. or until the aubergine begins to soften, with lid on pan – (a little vegetable stock or water may need to be added to prevent sticking).

Add the sun dried tomatoes and herbs and stir. Remove the aubergine cases from the oven and pack with the prepared filling. Mix the breadcrumbs and cheese together and put on top. Return to the oven and bake, uncovered, for 10–15mins. or until the topping is crisp and brown. Serve hot with rice, fresh bread or salad.

Lazy Cook tips – *I find a grapefruit knife a useful tool for removing aubergine flesh. Nuts or dried apricots could also be added to the filling. Aubergine has a good protein content so additional protein fillings eg. meat or poultry, should be kept to the minimum. An excellent vegetarian recipe.*

Baked Marrow – *serves 6–8*

> 1 fat marrow
> 450g (1lb) cooked minced beef – recipe on page 109
> 4 tomatoes
> sprinkling of sugar
> little oil
> sprinkling of herbs
> freshly ground pepper

Set oven at gas 6/200°C/180°C fan/Aga roasting oven, 3rd runner down.

Wash the marrow then cut in half lengthways and remove and discard the centre seeds. Score the marrow flesh and place, cut side up, in a shallow ovenproof dish or roasting tin. Fill the cavity with the cooked minced beef and top with tomato slices brushed with oil and seasoned with a sprinkling of sugar, freshly ground pepper and chopped herbs (fresh or dried). Add boiling water to come 1/4 way up the dish, cover with foil and bake in the preset oven for 45mins–1 hr. or until the marrow is tender (test with a metal skewer). Remove the foil towards the end of cooking to brown the tomatoes a little. Serve with fresh bread, rice or couscous.

Lazy Cook tips – *a good recipe for feeding a crowd of hungry youngsters.*

Baked Swede

1 whole swede
4–6 wafer thin slices Parma or Black Forest ham
6 sun dried tomatoes and a little oil
1 lemon

Peel and chop the swede into small chunks. Add to boiling water and boil, with lid on pan, until softened. Strain off the cooking liquid (keep to use as vegetable stock), mash the swede. Remove all fat from the ham and tear each slice into strands and add to the mashed swede. Remove the tomatoes from the oil and cut with scissors directly into the swede, including a little of the oil in which they have been preserved. Mix all together before putting into a vegetable dish and scattering with fresh lemon juice and serve.

Lazy cook tips – *please refer to notes on preparation of vegetables, page 139, to prepare the swede. Keep the liquid strained from cooking the swede to use as vegetable stock – when cold store in a refrigerator and use within 3–4 days. Swede is one of my favourite winter flavours but it is so rarely promoted. I do hope you will try this and experiment by adding your own favourite flavours.*

Celeriac and Parsnip Mash

450g (1lb) parsnip
450g (1lb) celeriac
freshly grated nutmeg
single cream – *optional*

Top and tail and scrub the parsnip before cutting into chunks. Peel the celeriac and cut into chunks. Put both into a pan containing a little boiling water, put lid on pan and boil until softened (approx 10mins.) Drain off the cooking liquid (keep for stock), season the vegetables with freshly grated nutmeg and mash. Stir in a little single cream and serve hot.

Lazy Cook tips – *the vegetables should be roughly equal in weight.*

Courgette Bake – *serves 4–6*

8 courgettes
1 jar sundried tomatoes in oil
freshly ground black papper
grated nutmeg
shavings of cheese – a variety of flavours

Set oven at gas 6/200°C/180°C fan/Aga roasting oven, 2nd runner down.

Wash and top and tail the courgettes and slice across into roughly 1cm (½″) slices before adding to a little boiling water and boil for no longer than 1min. Remove from pan using a slotted spoon and put into a shallow ovenproof dish. Season with freshly ground black pepper and grated nutmeg. Remove the tomatoes from the jar using kitchen tongs and dab with kitchen roll to remove some of the oil. Scatter the tomatoes, (cut with scissors if you wish), over the courgettes. Top with shavings of cheese and bake in the pre-set oven, uncovered, for 10–15mins. Serve with hot or cold meats or fish; with rice or pasta tossed in a little oil from the jar of sundried tomatoes and freshly chopped herbs.

Lazy Cook tips – *this is a very colourful dish and full of good flavours. A good way of using up ends of cheese – stilton, brie, cheddar, parmesan etc. Prepare in advance, adding the cheese immediately before baking and bake until hot throughout.*

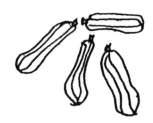

Creamy Potato Flan – *serves 4–6*

1 ready cooked pastry case
225g (8oz) cooked potato
freshly grated nutmeg
mixed herbs – fresh or dried
1 tbls. capers
1 tbls. pitted black olives
2 large eggs
2 teas. Dijon mustard
150ml (5fl.oz) single cream
tomato slices

Set oven at gas 4/180°C/160°C fan/Aga baking oven 3rd runner down.

Put the pastry case on a baking tray. Slice the potato thickly and pack into the pastry case. Season with freshly grated nutmeg and herbs, and scatter with capers and olives, before topping with tomato slices. Whisk the eggs, warm the cream and mustard and add to the eggs and whisk again before pouring (through a sieve), over the flan ingredients. Bake in the pre-set oven for 20–30mins. or until set. Remove from oven and serve hot, warm or cold with salad or vegetables, rice or couscous.

Lazy Cook tips – *this is an excellent way of using up cooked potato. If you do not wish to make it into a flan, put the ingredients into a pie dish and bake as for the flan.*

Floret Bake – *to serve 4–6*

1 medium sized cauliflower
1 head of calibrese of a similar size to the cauliflower
100–175g (4–6oz) Shropshire Blue or Stilton cheese
75g (3oz) jumbo oats

Set oven at gas 6/200°C/180°C fan/Aga roasting oven, 2nd runner down.

Break the cauliflower and calibrese into small florets and wash. Add to roughly 300ml (10fl.oz) boiling water and boil, with lid on pan for 2–5mins. or until they begin to soften. Remove from heat and using a slotted spoon put the florets into a shallow ovenproof dish and add half the cooking water (approx. 150ml (5fl.oz)). Grate or crumble the cheese and mix with the oats before spreading over the florets. Bake in the preset oven for 10–15mins. Serve straight from the oven. Alternatively put under a hot grill, reducing the temperature after the first few minutes. Serve as a vegetarian meal with rice or pasta, or with meat, poultry or fish recipes.

Lazy Cook tips – *a mixture of leftover bits of cheese can be used, and as little or as much as suits your diet. The florets can be cooked in advance and stored, covered, in a refrigerator or cold larder, store the cooking liquid separately, (use within 3–4 days). Allow 20–30mins. to reheat from cold.*

Marrow Rings with Spinach and Goats Cheese – makes 6

1 vegetable marrow
450g (1lb) cooked spinach – recipe on page 176
freshly grated nutmeg
6 slices goats cheese

Set oven at gas 6/200°C/180°C fan/Aga roasting oven, 2nd runner down.

Cut the marrow into 6 rings each approx. 2cm/1″ thick. Remove and discard the centre pith and seeds before adding to boiling water and boil for 1–2mins. or until the marrow begins to soften, remove from pan and place in a shallow ovenproof dish. Fill each marrow cavity with cooked spinach, season with freshly grated nutmeg and top with a slice of goats cheese. Put into the pre-set oven until the cheese has melted and browned on top. Remove from heat and serve with salad for a light meal, or as a vegetable accompaniment to meat or fish.

Marrow and Tomato Bake – *serves 6–8*

1 marrow
fresh sage – chopped
1 x 400gm tin chopped tomatoes
pinch sugar
freshly ground white pepper
100g (4oz) cheese

Set oven gas 6/200°C/180°C fan/Aga roasting oven, 3rd runner down.

Wash and top and tail the marrow before cutting into half lengthways. Remove the centre seeds and discard. Slice each half marrow into three lengths and cut each of these into slices approximately 5mm (¼″) thick. Cook in a little boiling water for about a minute to begin the softening process then, using a slotted spoon, put them into a large shallow ovenproof dish and scatter with chopped sage leaves. Cover with the tinned tomatoes and juice, add a good pinch of sugar and season with freshly ground pepper. Shred or grate the cheese over the top. Bake, uncovered, in the pre-set oven for 20–30mins. or until hot and bubbly. Serve hot with a summer roast.

Lazy Cook tips — *this has become one of the most favourite summer vegetables I serve. It can be prepared in advance and stored, covered, in a refrigerator or cold larder in readiness for heating. Use a mixture of cheeses, including a little Stilton for extra flavour – it is a good way of using up all the bits. Mix the cheese with breadcrumbs for an alternative topping – keep a supply of dried breadcrumbs (brown or white) in store (recipe on page 151), it makes the preparation of this and many other recipes so much quicker.*

Medley of Summer Vegetables

carrots – leave whole with tails on and a fraction of the tops
french beans – leave whole
mangetout or sugarsnap peas
courgettes – top and tail and cut across to form oval shapes
a smear of butter – *optional*
freshly grated parsley
freshly grated nutmeg

Boil approx 425ml (15fl.oz) water in a large pan. Cook all the prepared vegetables in the order in which they are listed removing them with a slotted spoon before adding the next. Arrange individually on to a large hot serving dish or plate, covering with foil to keep hot. Finally smear the top with butter, scatter the carrots with parsley and season the courgettes with grated nutmeg.

Lazy Cook tips – at the end of cooking there should be very little water remaining. I find this an attractive way of presenting summer vegetables and serving them all on one large plate avoids the clutter of lots of individual dishes. To serve with a cold summer buffet mix all the cooked vegetables together and stir in a little oil and some freshly chopped herbs.

Parsnip and Orange Mash

450g (1lb) approx. parsnips
1 tbls. fresh orange juice

Top and tail and scrub the parsnips before cutting into chunks then add to a little boiling water and boil, with lid on pan, until soft (approx. 5–10mins.) Drain off the cooking liquid, add 1 tbls. fresh orange juice to the parsnips and mash. Serve hot with meat or poultry, or as part of a vegetarian meal.

Lazy Cook tips – always keep water drained from cooked vegetables to use as stock. Store when cold in a fridge and use within 2 days. A refreshing combination of flavours.

Potatoes Dressed with Oil and Chives

    new potatoes – cooked
    oil
    chives

Scrub the skins before boiling the potatoes. Drain the liquid from the pan. Snip chives directly on to the hot potatoes in the pan (using scissors), and add a little oil. Stir with 2 wooden spoons before pouring into a serving bowl. Serve hot, warm or cold.

Lazy Cook tips – *a delicious way to serve the first seasons new potatoes.*

Potato Gratinée – *serves 4–6*

    900g (2lb) potatoes
    garlic – *optional*
    50g (2oz) butter – melted
    nutmeg – freshly grated

Set oven at gas 6/200°C/180°C fan/Aga roasting oven, 2nd runner down.

Lightly oil a shallow ovenproof dish. Peel the potatoes, slice very thinly and layer with the garlic into the prepared dish. Pour melted butter over the top and season with freshly grated nutmeg. Bake in the pre-set oven for 30mins to 1hr. depending on the quantity being baked. Serve hot from the oven.

Roasted Parsnips and Aubergine

    450g (1lb) parsnips
    1 large aubergine
    oil
    1 lemon – juice and zest

Set oven at gas 6/200°C/180°C fan/Aga roasting oven, 2nd runner down.

Top and tail and scrub the parsnips and cut in half and then into quarters or chunky lengths. Put into a pan and cover with cold water, bring to boil, remove from heat and strain off the cooking liquid. Put 2 tbls. oil into a roasting tin and put in the pre-set oven until it is hot. Meanwhile, wash and top and tail the aubergine and cut into lengths of a similar size to the parsnips. Put both into the pan and brush all over with the hot oil, return to the oven and roast for 20–30mins. or until both vegetables have browned and softened. Remove from oven, put into a hot serving dish, squeeze the juice from half the lemon over and scatter with lemon zest before serving with a roast or as part of a vegetarian meal.

Lazy Cook tips – *remove the zest from the lemon before cutting it in half. A good contrast of flavours and colours. Use the parsnip stock in other recipes, when cold store it in a refrigerator or cold larder and use within 4 days.*

Roasted Vegetables with Camargue Rice
– *serves 4*

> 225g (8oz) camargue rice
> 1–2 tbls. oil
> 1 large fat aubergine
> 4–6 peppers (assorted colours)
> several sprigs of fresh rosemary
> 1 jar sundried tomatoes

Cook the rice following the recipe on page 173.

Set oven at gas 6/200°C/180°C fan /Aga roasting oven 2nd runner down.

Heat the oil in a roasting tin in the pre-set oven. Prepare the peppers by removing and discarding the stalk and inside seeds then cut each pepper into quarters. Put into the hot oil, skin side up. and lightly oil the skin side only. Top and tail the aubergine and slice lengthways into

5–6 slices. Put into the tin with the peppers and lightly brush all over with the remaining oil, scatter rosemary sprigs over the top. Bake in the pre-set oven for 15–20mins. or until the vegetables begin to brown and soften, remove from oven. Remove the rosemary sprigs from the stalks (discard stalks), add sundried tomatoes (drained from the oil) and the cooked rice and stir together. Pile into a hot dish and serve hot or cold with salad, meat or fish.

Lazy Cook tips *– cook the peppers and aubergine in the oil from the jar of sundried tomatoes – keep remainder to use in other recipes. The cooking juices in the roasting tin will add moisture and flavour. An excellent vegetarian recipe.*

Serving Suggestions *– serve hot or cold, with salad, meat or fish.*

To Cook Rice

250g (8oz) rice – wholemeal, black, camargue, white

Put the rice into a sieve and wash it under a cold running tap before adding to a pan containing 1ltr (1³/₄pt) boiling water. Stir well, bring to a simmer, put lid on pan and simmer gently for 20–30mins. or until the rice is of a nutty texture. Pour back into a sieve and rinse thoroughly under a cold running tap, drain well. Use as directed in a recipe or store, covered, in a refrigerator or cold larder. Use within 3 days.

Lazy Cook tips *– American long grain white rice will cook in a shorter time, test after 10mins. The cooked grains should remain whole, tender and separate. If the cooked rice is to be served hot rinse it in boiling water poured from a kettle.*

Roasted Winter Vegetables

potatoes – peel and cut into large chunks
pumpkin – peel, remove and discard centre seeds,
    cut into thick slices
parsnips – top and tail, scrub, cut into chunky lengths
small onions – skin and cut off root growth
2 tbls. oil
course grain salt

Set oven at gas 6/200°C/180°C fan/Aga roasting oven, high runner.

Put all the prepared vegetables into a large pan, cover with cold water, put lid on pan and bring to boil. Strain off all cooking liquid. While the vegetables are cooking, heat the oil in a large roasting tin. Put the drained vegetables into the roasting tin and spoon the oil over. Roast in the pre-set oven for 45mins.–1hr. or until browning and crisp. Put into a hot serving dish and scatter with a little course grain salt to serve.

Lazy Cook tips – *the vegetable water can be used for making gravy or when cold frozen in bags for future use in soups and sauces. Place all the vegetables cut side up to roast. Prepare and cook the quantity needed.*

Saucy Leeks

450g (1lb) leeks
few good pinches ground clove
40g (1½oz) butter
25g (1oz) plain flour
freshly ground white pepper
150ml (5fl.oz) milk
75g (3oz) Shropshire Blue or Stilton cheese

Set oven at gas 6/200°C/180°C fan/Aga roasting oven, 3rd runner down.

Top and tail the leeks then cut, including the green end, into rings approx. 2cm (1") lengths. Wash well under a cold running tap. Boil

174

approx. 150ml (5fl.oz) water in a large pan, add the prepared leeks and boil, with lid on pan, for a minute or until they begin to soften, strain off the liquid and keep, put the leeks into a shallow ovenproof dish and season with ground clove. Melt the butter over a gentle heat in the pan, stir in the flour and cook for 1–2mins. or until a paste is formed. Add the reserved liquid from the cooked leeks and the milk and stir until it boils and begins to thicken. Remove from heat, season with freshly ground white pepper then pour over the leeks. Scatter crumbled, sliced, or grated cheese on top and bake in the pre-set oven until hot and bubbling. Serve straight from the oven with a roast or other cooked meat, poultry or fish. A great vegetarian recipe – serve with rice, pasta, couscous or warm bread or rolls.

Lazy Cook tips – *the sauce should not be of too thick a consistency, add more milk if necessary, or a little single cream. Any left-over bits of cheese can be used in this recipe. See also, Saucy Onions and Saucy Beans below.*

Saucy Beans

Follow the recipe for Saucy Leeks (page 174) using broad bean pods in place of leeks. Omit the clove and scatter the partly cooked bean pods with shredded cooked ham before topping with sauce.

Lazy Cook tips – *buy young, small broad beans whenever possible. These can be topped and tailed, cut into approx. 2cm (1″) lengths and cooked. The flavour is different from the cooked pods but still good and saves discarding the skins.*

Saucy Onions

Follow the recipe for Saucy Leeks (page 174) using onions in place of leeks. Skin the onions and cut into thick rings or into quarters. Omit the clove and scatter the partly cooked onions with several good pinches of dried sage before topping with the sauce.

Spicy Potato Mash – *serves 4*

450–700g (1–1½lb) potatoes – boiled
25–50g (1–2oz) butter
little milk to soften
½ ring black pudding

Peel the potatoes and cut into small chunks. Add to a pan of boiling water and boil, with lid on pan, until they soften. Strain off the liquid, add the butter and mash until smooth, adding a little milk to soften the texture if necessary. Crumble the black pudding into the mash and stir. Serve hot.

Spinach – to cook

Wash the leaves in cold water (including the stalks if the spinach is young). Drain well before putting into a pan and cooking over a gentle heat for a few minutes, lid on pan, until the leaves have softened and wilted. Remove from heat and strain off and keep any juices. Cut up the cooked leaves with scissors (or in a food processor) season with freshly grated nutmeg and serve.

Lazy Cook tips – if cooking a large quantity, turn the leaves during cooking using kitchen tongs to separate and cook evenly. Can be cooked and stored in a covered container in a refrigerator or cold larder. Use within 4 days – a most useful cooked ingredient to have in store. To reheat, melt a knob of butter in a pan, add the cooked spinach and stir over a gentle heat. Any stock from cooking should be used in other recipes, when cold store in a refrigerator or cold larder and use within 4 days. If fresh spinach is not available buy a bag of frozen and cook according to the directions on the packet – an excellent ingredient to keep in store.

Vegetable and Bacon Bake – *serves 4–6 people*

    selection of parsnips, sweet potato and celeriac weighing
        approx. 1kg (2¹/₄lb) in all
    1 large onion – skin and chop
    1 tbls. oil
    175g (6 oz) grated cheese
    150ml (5 oz) double cream (or a small carton of natural yoghurt)
    freshly ground white pepper
    ¹/₄ teas. medium curry powder
    2 tbls. jumbo oats (or fresh breadcrumbs)
    8 slices lean rindless streaky bacon

Set oven gas 6/200°C/180°C fan/Aga roasting oven, 2nd runner down.

Peel the sweet potato and celeriac, top and tail and scrub the parsnip and cut all into small chunks before boiling in water to cover until softened. Meanwhile, heat the oil in a large frying or sauté pan, add the prepared onion and 5 rashers of the bacon cut into small pieces and cook until softening. Strain the liquid from the cooked vegetables. Mash the vegetables together before adding to the cooked onion mixture. Add 100g (4oz) of the grated cheese and the cream, season with pepper and curry powder and mix together. Turn on to a lightly oiled baking tray and shape like a cake approx. 25cm (10″) in diameter and stick the remaining bacon rashers round the sides. Mix the remaining cheese with the oats and scatter on top. Bake in the pre-set oven for 20–30mins. or until hot and bubbly. To serve cut into slices and serve with fresh bread, rice or couscous. A delicious savoury meal and very filling – a good family meal.

Lazy Cook tips – *if preferred all the bacon, cut into small pieces, can be cooked with the onion and the prepared bake can be put into a pie dish to cook with the cheese and breadcrumb mixture on top. A selection of cheeses can be used, I recommend Cheddar, Stilton and Double Gloucester for good flavour and colour.*

Vegetable Rolls – *makes 4*

4 large spring cabbage leaves
2 large flat mushrooms – thickly slice
1 yellow pepper – slice into batons
8 spring onions – cut in half
sage, mint and parsley leaves
freshly ground black pepper
mushroom ketchup

Lay the cabbage leaves flat, cut out the thick centre stalk and fold the leaf to close the gap. Top each prepared leaf with equal slices of mushroom, pepper and spring onions and a few sage, mint and parsley leaves. Season with freshly ground black pepper and a dash of mushroom ketchup before rolling up tightly and securing with a wooden cocktail stick. Boil about 1cm (½″) water in a sauté or large frying pan, add the prepared rolls, bring to a simmer, put lid on pan and simmer for 5–10mins. or until the ingredients have softened – test with a skewer. Remove rolls from pan and keep warm. Add 150ml (5fl.oz) concentrated orange juice to the pan juices, and a tablespoon chopped sage, mint and parsley. Boil to reduce by half. To serve, remove the skewers and serve on individual hot plates or arrange on one large hot serving plate. Pour a little of the sauce over each and serve the remainder separately.

Lazy Cook tips – place some of the filling ingredients so that they protrude from the ends of the rolls. Top up with more boiling water during simmering if necessary. Can be steamed or, if serving with a roast, can be cooked in the oven for 15–20mins.

Store Cupboard

The choice of store cupboard is a personal one but in addition to the basics, dairy products and perishables, I recommend the following items which you may choose to keep in store and which will assist your conversion to Lazy cooking. Buy **Fairtrade** products whenever possible.

Anchovy essence
Anchovy fillets preserved in oil
Artichokes in oil – jars
Bayleaves – dried, whole
Cans concentrated orange juice
Capers in vinegar
Charbonnel et Walker, Chocolat Charbonnel (ready grated chocolate)
Chocolate – bitter, white
Ciabatta loaf – store in freezer
Cider vinegar
Cocktail gherkins
Cocktail onions
Condensed soups – chicken and mushroom
Cornichons – pickled
Course grain salt
Dijon mustard
Dried breadcrumbs
Dried pasta
Dried mushrooms
Dried tarragon and other herbs
English mustard powder or ready made
Fresh yeast – freeze
Frozen fruits and berries – in freezer
Frozen ready-rolled puff pastry
Frozen short-crust pastry

Gelatine crystals, cubes or leaf gelatine
Ginger wine
Gravy browning
Ground clove
Ground white pepper
Herbes de Provence
Honey – runny and set
Horseradish cream
HP Sauce
Marmite
Mint jelly
Moutarde de meaux – Pommery
Mushroom ketchup
Nutmegs
Orange flower water
Oven chips – in freezer
Piccalilli
Pickled walnuts
Pitted black olives
Potato crisps
Prawns in shells – in freezer
Ready-baked pastry cases
Ready-baked sponge flan cases
Rice – wholemeal, black, camargue, white
Rose water
Shredded suet
Sliced bread – in freezer
Stem ginger
Sundried tomato paste
Sundried tomato purée
Sundried tomatoes (jars in oil)
Sundried tomatoes (dried)
Tapenade – (olive paste) – in jars
Tins – salmon, sardines, mackerel
Tomato ketchup
Vanilla extract – twice the strength of essence
Vanilla ice cream
Worcestershire sauce

Recommended Equipment

Basics

In addition to a chopping board and a sharp knife, generally known as the tools of the trade, other basic items might include baking trays, wire cooling trays, a grater, lemon squeezer, various spoons and ladles. A measuring jug, wooden spoons and spatulas. The choice is very much a personal one but many years practice has proved to me that using the right tool makes the preparation of ingredients much easier and quicker. More major purchases include a food processor – an invaluable buy for a Lazy Cook, and an electric hand whisk.

Serving dishes and plates

Purchase a variety of colourful ovenproof ceramic dishes of varying sizes and shapes, also serving dishes and plates. Should you be fortunate enough to have inherited them, take Granny's lovely old plates and dishes out of the cupboard and use them to show off your meals.

Pots and Pans

Here I stress the importance of putting 'quality' before 'quantity'. Good pots and pans can last for years, if not a lifetime with careful handling, which is not extravagant, even at today's prices.

I recommend pans that can be used on a hob and then put into the oven and from which the cooked meal can be served, or a sauce can be made using the cooking juices. This saves a lot of time and washing up. My favourite pans are a large sauté pan with a lid; heavy based saucepans; enamelled cast-iron casseroles and shallow baking dishes, with or without lids, (a tin plate or foil will substitute for a lid).

Hob Temperatures

Gentle simmer – an occasional bubble
Simmer – a more regular bubble
Boil – constant bubbles
Rapid boil – constant bubbles rising in pan

Aga owners should start the simmering process on the hobs then transfer the pan to the simmering oven.

Oven Temperatures

These can vary considerably and the temperatures given below, and the ones quoted in the recipes in this book, should be used as guidelines and adjusted according to your cooker. Aga owners please refer to your instruction manual.

Temperature	Gas	ºC	Fan (ºC)
Warm	1–2	120–150	100–130
Moderate–Simmering	3–4	160–180	140–160
Baking	4–5	180–190	160–170
Roasting	6–7	200–220	180–200

Weights and Measures

as used in recipes in this book

Dry measurements

25g	=	1oz
50g	=	2oz
100g	=	4oz
175g	=	6oz
225g	=	8oz
450g	=	1lb
700g	=	1½lb
900g	=	2lb
1kg	=	2lb 4oz
1¾kg	=	4lb
teas.	=	teaspoon
desst.	=	dessertspoon
tbls.	=	tablespoon

Liquid measurements

100ml	=	4fl.oz
150ml	=	5fl.oz (1 gill)
300ml	=	10fl.oz
425ml	=	15fl.oz
600ml	=	1 pint
1ltr	=	1¾ pints
1¾ltr	=	3 pints

Main Index

C

D

G

H

I

K

L

P